ENDEAVOUR AT CAPE HORN

by

John Selwyn Gilbert

Endeavour at Cape Horn

XIX

To view the photos in colour and additional maps and materials go to:

EndeavourAtCapeHorn.blogspot.com

The password is E'sswbh

JSG Productions, Ltd.,

44, Wellington Street,

London, WC2E 7BD

Enquiries - please contact John Selwyn Gilbert,

email: JohnSelwynGilbert@yahoo.com

telephone: 07831 811076

This book is for my grandchildren, my shipmates and in memory of my mother, who would have enjoyed the craic.

THE ENDEAVOUR REPLICA

Light airs, all sail set, Torres Strait, 2001

**I know nothing that can give a better notion of infinity
and eternity than the being upon the sea in a little
vessel with nothing in sight but yourself and the whole
hemisphere.**

Samuel Pepys, Secretary of the Navy and diarist

TABLE OF CONTENTS

THE GREAT STORM

That was the scariest night of all.

The whole watch huddled down below, not knowing what was happening. Just two or three of us out on deck, because it was so rough. We slept, of course. We were very very tired. We dozed and grunted and snored and scratched ourselves through our heavy oilskins. I snored, I think. The others told me that I always snored.

"Maybe," I said, "I can't do anything about it. I never hear myself."

"You're lucky," said Kate bitterly.

She was nineteen at the time. I was nearly sixty.

We couldn't read, because there was no light. We couldn't talk, because there were people round us in their hammocks, trying to sleep, people on different watches, with different obligations and duties.

Also, I am not sure we had anything new left to say to each other by that time. We had been at sea continuously together for more than thirty days.

Just crawling in there, into 'the Marines', the cramped area between decks, like a wooden cave, where Captain Cook's seagoing soldiers used to sleep, settling ourselves by the ladders that led up onto the deck, trying to get in there without disturbing anyone - that was a performance in itself in our heavy foul-weather gear. And then all we could do was fall back uncomfortably into a half sleep. We were quite happy to be silent, to be at rest. We were very apprehensive.

Suddenly I was called. I had to go up there, onto the deck. Something had gone wrong, one of my watchmates had been hurt - that's what I heard - I had to go up there. In a hurry, in an emergency - into sixty or seventy knots of wind, a big Southern Ocean storm, into a situation where the ship's officers wouldn't let all of the watch on the deck because it was too dangerous to be up there. An interesting moment.

I went up onto the deck that night like a Spanish bull entering the arena, lumbering stupidly, looking side to side to find out what was necessary, to see what was happening. I was very determined and I thought it was an emergency. I was charged up.

The sight of the ocean made me sensible, made me consider.

A big storm at sea changes everything - the air fills with spume and spray - the shape of the waves changes - the way the boat moves is so sensational, so elemental, that you can't compare it with anything you've ever seen or experienced before. Big storms at sea remind you that you are very ordinary and extremely unimportant and small - a scrap of dust in a very large universe - you go out there on deck wanting to fight, wanting to confront the danger and do something and take control, but that is not how it works .... a big storm at sea is something else.

You have to accept it.

The waves coming at us with the wind were immense - forty or more feet between peak and trough. Some of them were breaking beside us (which is when they get most dangerous). The whole world was grey and bitter and intense and severe and immensely beautiful. I will never forget how spectacularly beautiful it was. You could see nothing ahead, which didn't matter. We were several thousand miles from a shipping lane or anywhere you would expect to encounter a vessel. We were posting a lookout (just one, instead of the usual two) almost as a technicality. That night, we were on our own with the weather, with the storm.

It was, as I said, elemental.

That night, I went up and took over the helm in a hurry. JP had been steering and he had been hurt when his helm-mate had lost control for a minute. JP had been thrown right over the helm , the wheel, and off it. He was OK - shaken - but OK. The wheel on Endeavour is almost six foot in diameter. It had kicked back so savagely that JP had been thrown the whole way across the deck.

We were hove to, head to wind, trying not to go anywhere.

In that situation, all the helmsmen have to do is to point the ship's head against the direction of the sails. The ship is made to contradict herself, the rudder taking her in one direction the sails in another, which means she will stay locked head to wind, just drifting backwards. It should have been easy but that was a big, big storm, that night. Force Eleven, for anyone who know the Beaufort scale – that's impressive, memorable. Just this side of a hurricane. About seventy knots of wind across the unprotected deck where we had to work. Very dangerous indeed.

We were somewhere off the western side of Chile, pitching through thirty or forty feet fore and aft, rolling at least 100 degrees from side to side. The cannons in the waist of the ship, the centre, were dipping in the water and nobody could walk down there even with the safety lines rigged - there was too much water coming on board. The lookout wasn't on the bow - he or she had to be up on the quarterdeck and it was still pretty wet and dangerous up there. You often had to duck.

In those conditions, the waves are grey and bright and white and utterly unpredictable; you can never tell which wave is going to come on board or when; and the spray on top of them will blow off , blow around all over the place; and it is pitch-black night as well. You couldn't see much at all, even people beside you.

I could understand why the ship's officers wouldn't let the whole of the watch up on deck that night. The conditions were so fierce and thick that you could lose somebody over the side and not even realize they had gone until you called the roll at the end of the watch.

In the 36 hours it continued, the storm carried us nearly 200 miles to the north in exactly the direction we did not want to go. But we were lucky; none of the storms we encountered went on for more than 48 hours and, in that area, storms can go on for weeks rather than hours. Then, once the storm had abated, we had to claw back down towards the Horn and out from the Chilean coast so that we wouldn't get embayed, pinned against that rocky coast by the prevailing wind and currents.

An old-fashioned square rigger like Endeavour simply will not sail upwind - she may manage to sail across the wind in reasonable conditions but, in a big wind the leeway is stupendous. The ship goes sideways very fast, probably into trouble.

If you get embayed there, pinned against the Chilean coast by the prevailing westerlies, you are in danger even if you have big engines to help you. We only had one useable engine, all the way across the Pacific from New Zealand, so we couldn't afford to get too close to the coast.

An eighteenth or nineteenth century mariner, navigating just with a sextant and a compass, with no engines at all, needed to be very careful indeed if he approached Cape Horn from the west.

His ship was extremely vulnerable to navigational errors and it was almost impossible to know his position accurately a century or more before GPS became available.

When we reached Cape Horn, we had been 39 days out of sight of land and we had not seen the sun or any star for 18 days.

*****

INTRODUCTION

The Endeavour Replica, from Australia, is a beautiful square rigged bark, a re-creation of the ship that Captain Cook commanded on his first great voyage of exploration. She was built from the original dockyard plans drawn up nearly 250 years ago.

Cook and his 93 officers, crew and supernumeraries left Deptford, in Britain on 26th. August, 1768. More than 50 of them returned safely on 13th. July, 1771.

In their three years away, Cook and his crew discovered and surveyed the whole of the east coast of Australia, from Botany Bay to Cape York.

They claimed Australia for the British crown and, less than a generation later, British people started to colonise Australia and to transform it.

They found out where the Great Barrier Reef is and survived to tell the tale (but only just).

They were the first British explorers to circumnavigate New Zealand and they built a temporary observatory in Tahiti to observe the transit of Venus across the sun and to take part in a ground-breaking international scientific experiment.

Cook brought most of his crew home alive in spite of malaria and dysentery, 'the bloody flux', which they picked up when they called at Batavia in the Dutch East Indies, (now called Jakarta in Indonesia).

It was an extraordinary triumph and the Endeavour replica, built and created by Australians, commemorates the achievment.

Endeavour functions as a museum ship when tied up in port but, out at sea, even in very heavy weather, she is one of the most effective vessels you can imagine.

Peter Weir, the film director, spent time on board Endeavour when he was planning "Master and Commander, the Far Side of the World".

He wrote that Endeavour is ".... the only replica vessel afloat that has a period-accurate lower deck .... you live as they did. You sleep in hammocks and work watches and go up the rigging ... it's just work, sleep, eat ... work, sleep eat. And you're working in a team."

He put a two-man film crew and a huge Panavision camera on board Endeavour to capture film footage of storms and the sea as she sailed around Cape Horn.

His crew filmed from the open deck of Endeavour, in nightmarish conditions, and I definitely recognized some of the biggest, wettest waves in 'Master and Commander', especially in the great storm when a boy is left to drown to save the ship.

I spent a total of 166 days at sea on Endeavour in 2001 and 2002 and sailed more than 18,000 miles.

When I was not too tired (and I was regularly exhausted), there was time for reflection, for study and for experimenting with some of the old-fashioned navigational techniques which I still find fascinating.

But I also got very interested in the people who sailed with me.

*****

Pete the Fish (Peter Deakin)
The day we reached Cape Horn

CAPTAIN JAMES COOK, F.R.S.

James Cook, from the National Maritime Museum Collection

Endeavour in dry dock

Built like a barrel, to carry cargo, she also rolls like a barrel most of the time. She is a very valiant vessel in rough seas and difficult conditions but horribly uncomfortable for anyone with a tendency to suffer sea sickness - that is, most normal people.

SAILING THE BARK

Endeavour is hard work. She always will be. There were a lot of improvements in the design, construction and operation of sailing ships in the 150 or more years after the Earl of Pembroke was built as a collier in Whitby, in 1764, and sold to the Admiralty and re-built and re-named Endeavour for Captain Cook to navigate her to Tahiti and then to go on and venture into unknown lands and seek scientific information and, if possible, new colonies, rich new territories, to add to the British Empire.

The later ships had smaller sails and eventually a lot less need for manpower. By the end of the nineteenth century, there were steam-driven winches and mechanical devices which could help haul up the halyards and tension up the sheets. The big fast nineteenth century tea clippers like the celebrated Cutty Sark carried relatively small crews.

Working and living on Endeavour doesn't reflect any of these improvements, which is fascinating and something of a challenge if you are interested in how old ships worked and what the problems of managing them might have been.

N.A.M. Rodger's book, 'The Wooden World', is a delight to read and will tell you more about the eighteenth century British navy than you can possibly imagine or remember. It is the rock upon which most studies of that period are built.

If you read Rodger's book and go sailing on Endeavour (even for a few days) you will start to understand what Captain Cook and Nelson were up against and how they worked, lived and died.

Endeavour, with all sails set, in the Torres Strait in 2001

On Endeavour, to set just one of the seven principal square sails on board takes about 20 people, which is more than one full watch by the time the lookouts have been posted, the wheel manned and the day's temporary galley assistant has gone to start his or her labours.

It takes more than forty minutes. To set all the sails takes most of the ship's company much of a day. Even furling one of the staysails can be hideously difficult when the ship is pitching and rolling.

There are ten staysails, spritsails and jibs to deal with in all. As we struggled with the main mast staysail, the most awkward sail on the ship, Bernard and I used to speculate repeatedly on what extremely wicked sins we must have committed in our previous lives to be made to suffer so, in penance!

The biggest square sails on Endeavour, the main course and fore course, have more than a dozen lines attached, all of which need tending, hauling or belaying:

port and starboard sheets,

port and starboard tacks

port and starboard clews, bunts and reefs

port and starboard bowlines

port and starboard braces

port and starboard lifts

The main, foremast and mizzen mast topsails have halyards as well, to lift the topsail yards, which is the heaviest possible work on the ship. But the topsails do not have tacks, in opposition to their sheets.

Learning the ropes is one of the first things that voyage crew have to do when they come on board Endeavour. It's a real challenge. There are about 180 of them.

To my surprise (because I have a good memory for facts and documents and anything in writing) I found it very difficult to learn the ropes.

On the other hand, I always found it fairly easy to get to the right rope when we were actually working - it was the quizzes and line races on board which confused me. I could never put the names and positions of the lines satisfactorily together in my head though I could normally remember what they did and which way I had to run to reach them.

An unexpected difficulty and an odd confusion; but an additional insight into myself and my own weaknesses which, of course, is sometimes what the Endeavour experience is about - finding out about yourself and what you can do.

To raise the anchor by traditional methods, as we did on the BBC voyage in 2001, involved linking the anchor cable to a messenger cable attached to the capstan and recruiting twenty people or more to trudge round the capstan for two or more hours while 10 or 15 other people attached the messenger cable, temporarily and repeatedly, to the anchor cable with the nipping lines, short pieces of rope cut and prepared just for that purpose.

The 'nippers' (the ship's boys) ran the nipping lines back and forth from the capstan back to the bows to re-cycle them.

Virtually the whole ship's company had to be involved apart from Caroline, the cook, and her assistant and the ship's officers.

It was an introduction to another age, an age when manpower was very cheap indeed, when machines built of wood and powered only by canvas, British naval vessels, could carry vast quantities of state-of-the-art firepower half way round the globe, sometimes safely, sometimes reliably, sometimes they got back home, and they could - because of their firepower, discipline and organization- take possession of great tracts of land in the Southern Ocean, New Zealand and Australia, to name but two substantial tracts, with or without the agreement of the inhabitants.

I was surprised that the BBC series "The Ship", in which I took part, did not show and discuss more of the extraordinary skills that the crew and Captain of the Endeavour replica can deploy.

I was very impressed with all of them - as people and as craftsmen and women. They are remarkable. They remain good friends.

Andy Law (R), the carpenter at Cape Horn with his assistant, Tig.

The Captain when I sailed with Endeavour, Chris Blake, is a great man. He deserves his O.B.E.

The weird skills he deployed to motivate his (fast-changing) professional crews, to motivate and discipline his (paying) voyage crews as well, to keep the ship and its rigging in order - there are very few people in the world who could have kept all that together.

After that, he still had to sail Endeavour and to ensure we went in roughly the right direction, which he also did with great distinction and expertise.

The Captain loses his balance. A noteworthy event. He almost never did.

My first glimpse of Endeavour - at anchor, offshore, across a mangrove swamp

In August 2001, the BBC invited me to join Endeavour and to help to re-create the arcane system of navigation which Captain Cook used on his first famous voyage. We were going to sail the ship and navigate just as Cook had done, to forget the twenty first century completely. I sighted Endeavour for the first time, clutching my sextant, with a bunch of others also picked by the BBC for this unusual experimental voyage. We had marched through a mangrove swamp for what seemed like miles and, when we eventually arrived on the beach, we had to be laboriously transferred out to the ship, which was lying offshore at anchor, in two or three small rowing boats. It took all day so it was a sweaty and tedious experience and there was no water on the beach and no food. When I finally climbed on board Endeavour, I was shattered. And I looked round the crowded, claustrophobic little deck, littered with packages and luggage, lined with canons, ropes, cleats, rigging and thought: "this is wonderful, this is just what I have been waiting for all my life." I had always been mad about sailing. For years and years, bringing up my family, making films, I had no time to indulge my obsession. Now, my chance had come. As soon as the BBC voyage was over, a mere six weeks in duration, only a couple of thousand miles of sailing, I signed up to re-join the Endeavour, to attempt the sailor's Everest, to sail round Cape Horn not in a modern cruise ship or in a racing yacht but in one of the most beautiful square rigged vessels in the world. This is the story of what happened next.

The first leg

Fremantle, W. Australia, to Hobart in Tasmania - 2114 miles

4th. February, 2002 - Monday

It is 24 hours since we left the docks at Fremantle in bright sunshine, cheered on by 1,000 or more supporters on the quayside, garlanded with streamers, with bagpipes wailing from two stout tartan pipers in a large launch, with helicopters circling noisily overhead and a flotilla of small motor boats surrounding us rather too closely, so that we had to wave them vigorously away before we could fire all our four cannon as a salute, a farewell, for good luck.

The ship was crammed with unstored provisions, greasy with oil and dust from the dry dock where she had spent the last few weeks. We had all laboured mightily, the professional crew (from 5am) to get the ship back into the water, the rest of us (between 1230 and 1700) to get all the museum furniture quickly off the ship and vast quantities of flour, tinned butter, fruit, powdered milk, meat, vegetables, tallow and cordage somehow on board, a job which ought to have taken three days, not three hours. This process was not much assisted by the crowds of rubber neckers trying to jam up the quay as a mobile crane moved the big anchor into place, a huge tanker lorry backed up to load fuel and a refrigerated lorry backed up, from the opposite direction, to deliver the foodstuffs. It was a triumph to get going at all that night. We weren't really ready.

But to postpone departure would have been a terrible disapointment to the press, to the public, to the supernumeraries and voyage crew, all of whom had expected to board on Saturday and some of whom, failing to locate Endeavour at Victoria Quay, in Fremantle, because she was still miles away, at the Tennix yard, Henderson, had had a very panicky afternoon, trying to find out what was happening and where the ship and their fellow crew members had disappeared to and to catch up.

What followed our spectacular departure was a sublime anti-climax.

We motored, in circles, for a long time, off the Fremantle breakwater while the two big magnetic compasses in the stern were checked and adjusted. This would normally take an hour or so and needs to be done about every two years.

On this occasion it took four hours.

When the compasses had been well and truly swung, and the compass adjuster had issued his certificate and been ferried to shore, we motored north for an hour and anchored two kilometres off Cotesloe Beach, just opposite the Indiana Tea House, where I had eaten a farewell lunch two days previously.

At lunch on that sunny, hot Friday, my companion and I drank Sauvignon Blanc and ate exotic fish with garlic and jasmine rice and admired the wind-surfers and the kite boarders down in the waves below the restaurant, which overlooks the Indian ocean and has a spectacular view of the sunsets.

On board Endeavour, on the Sunday evening, there was no alcohol, but we ate grilled fish and salad and worked till midnight and I slung my hammock on Endeavour for the very first time.

This was my second voyage on Endeavour.

The first time I sailed on Endeavour I was one of the team of navigators, a privileged person with my own (minute) cabin. Now, I had no privacy whatsoever, just a locker about 18 inches square and 3 foot high for all my storage.

We anchored overnight. A couple of people stayed on duty each hour, to make sure that the ship was safe.

Between 0300 and 0400, I stood my first anchor watch with Stuart, a young gold miner from Perth with a wife and two children and a passion for wooden boats, which he restores lovingly in a large rented shed.

We dipped the bilges together, to find out if the ship was sinking. (She was not.) We checked the fridges and made sure the anchor wasn't dragging. (It was not.)

That was about all the excitement for the night, so Stuart and I talked.

He mines, he says, just for the money. There is little pleasure in it for him. He is also a qualified helicopter pilot but, to my surprise, he tells me he can earn more money in the mines than by flying.

In the gold mines, he works one week on days, one week on nights. They are twelve hour shifts. Then he is allowed a week off, to go home and see his family who live 1,000 kilometres south of where he works.

It is a hard, rather lonely existence; but Stuart makes a good living and supports his family handsomely.

"With a wife and two kids, no contest really, no choice. We need the money. I meant to stay two years and that was nine or ten years ago, so there's no way back now, there's no going back. I can't get back into the flying business now."

Stuart will only go to Hobart with the Bark – he can't afford the time to go further, to come all the way round Cape Horn. I think he would probably come if he could. His stock of youth is running out. His next big birthday will (I assume) be his fortieth. He wants an adventure or two, before it is too late.

Stuart is dark, lean and strong, with a lot of determination in his face and strength in his character.

The professional crew on Endeavour have devised a fitness test and exercise, which is to climb about twelve foot up a rope on deck (without using your legs) and kiss the big block at the top and then climb down, still without using your legs.

Stuart managed it as if it was easy.

He could probably have done it twice in succession.

Even when I was young, I doubt that I could have managed it at all.

After all the excitement of our departure, the first day on board was very quiet.

We spent the day cleaning, tidying and training. We listened to lectures on safety, sea-survival and steering. We climbed two of the three masts and out onto the bowsprit and even Martin Morant, a supernumerary who was then 71 years old, managed it fine, with a little encouragement and moral support.

We spent almost all day at anchor, waiting for some spares for a water pump to be delivered and finally got the anchor up and departed at 1900, under power. The wind was from the south or the south east, exactly the direction in which we needed to travel. There was no chance of sailing off the anchor, or even of setting sail once we had got going. This was a bit of a shame and set the pattern for the whole of the early passage.

Every morning, at the morning meeting on deck, Gary, standing in for Captain Chris Blake, or Glen, the first officer, would tell us where we were and where we were going.

That day, he said were going to head due south or a touch to the west of south to try to find our way into the bands of westerly winds which circle the planet 45 or so degrees south of the Equator. If we could get the westerlies behind us, we could scoot quickly east, towards Hobart.

We might even make up the day that we had lost regulating the compasses and waiting for the water pump spare to arrive.

Officers are often optimists.

In the forecastle, the ship's crew always tends to suspect that the voyage will be longer than the Captain says or wetter than he says, that the food will be worse than he says, that the hardships will be immeasurably harder than he says. A ship's crew is full of gossip, essentially suspicious - just like workmen anywhere, they always find something to complain about.

*****

9/11/01 - the BBC gang on the quarter deck of the Endeavour replica

Ten minutes later, the Captain told us what had happened in New York that morning.

Lucy cried and borrowed my dirty handkerchief.

I cried too.

5/2 - Tuesday

A decent night, in my hammock. But I snore loudly when I sleep on my back and I have not yet mastered the art of sleeping on my side in a hammock. So I feel sorry for those with hammocks close to me, within earshot.

Which is the whole of the voyage crew.

More than thirty people sleep in the eighteenth century deck, a space of about 40 feet by 30 The hammocks are within inches of each other, almost touching.

Sometimes they swing at different rates and bump each other.

I brought spare ear plugs to offer to anyone bothered by my snoring. However, I have not handed them out yet. No one has complained sufficiently loudly.

Today has been grossly busy. We've been under power most of the time, still heading west of south (200 degrees magnetic) but this morning we unfurled all the courses (the mainsails on each mast) and, pretty quickly, furled them up again.

This was arduous but quite satisfying.

I was on watch from 0800 so also stood a trick at the helm, gave an impromptu lesson in astro-navigation, ate lunch (ham and pea soup) then belted into cleaning the eighteenth century deck, which badly needed it.

When that was done, we had a fire drill and a lecture on fire hoses and the emergency fire pump – I am snatching a few moments to write this and do some navigational calculations before I go on deck. We are setting some sails at last. The wind is sharp and keen. I am scribbling this in the male heads (lavatories). I am due back on deck, on watch, in twenty minutes. We also have to eat.

5/2 - Tuesday (continued)

Off watch - 2000. Ate, slung hammock. Took sleeping pill – crashed.

"All hands! All hands!"

Three hours later, at 2330, the call over the Tannoy penetrating ear plugs, sleeping pill, blindfold.

I scrambled into warm gear, safety harness, reflective jacket. We needed to shorten sail as a matter of urgency – wind gusting force six, maybe seven, (25-30 knots), kicking up seas that broke vividly on Endeavour's blunt bow and beat against her stout sides.

Ship rolling horribly. People have started to be sick.

I went up onto the main topsail yard, looking down at the seas boiling white around the bows about seventy feet below, watching the black waves pounding us and looking up at the moonless sky pricked full of veiled stars with the familiar constellations all upside down, because I was viewing them from south of the Equator instead of from the north.

The wind grew fiercer, the delays (people were very inexperienced to work aloft in those conditions) less tolerable.

I was stuck out on the windward end of the yard (having finished my bit of the job) for 20 or 25 minutes while some unexpected hitches were sorted and some on the job training was administered nearer the mast.

The same happened on the main course yard, which we dealt with next. Eventually, we were dismissed below. I had tea with extra sugar and wrote these notes.

I will be back on watch in two hours, precisely.

The morning watch (0400 to 0800) was spectacular.
I wrote: "we are plunging southward under engine, with a wind of 30-33 knots (gusting 36-7) on our port beam. The seas it throws up fight mightily with the underlying currents and wave patterns from the west and the result is a confused and choppy wave pattern, with waves breaking in all directions. Some are huge — yawning like an abyss as you crest them — some short, sharp and vicious, snapping at the ship's heels like dogs around a bear."

The casualties are mounting up.

The Southern Ocean has begun to embrace us with its welcome. The beauty of the seascape, all fierce grey waves and bright white spray, leaves me full of wonder and delight.

But I am very very tired.

6/2 - Wednesday

The casualties so far:-

Simon, a tall, young Australian in his early twenties, with a pony tail and a taste for blues guitar, never even made it onto the ship. He failed his medical because of a recent break in his wrist, caused by a basketball injury. I was told he arranged to remove the cast prematurely, to try to fool the examining doctor, who was neither amused nor deceived. He may re-join at Hobart.

He was to have been one of the watchleaders.

Simon was deeply disapointed. Shocked. So was his mum who appeared proudly on the quayside to see him one more time, to say farewell before her son left for his long adventure. She found herself taking him home in the wagon.

Jennaya, sturdy and dark, 21 years old (but looks a little older), was to have been our watch leader but her knee went septic and won't heal properly. She can't climb the rigging and may have to leave the ship at Hobart.

On the second day of the voyage, to add insult to injury, she cut her finger badly and had to have stitches.

Before this month, she had never even been to a hospital, never had stitches. Now she is confined to her shared cabin and her leg is in a splint and she is forbidden even to walk around the ship.

Bones is a very skinny, almost skeletal young Australian – hence the nickname. He wears a cowboy hat over his 'beanie', a woollen hat which he mislaid the other day.

He was distraught until he found it.

He is often distraught about something.

Bones has an under-nourished fair moustache, a very young man's growth, and pale washed out blue eyes which look into you rather than at you. He is about 20, a farm worker and a keen Scout leader and a Seventh Day Adventist. He knows just how to fold the Australian national flag and how to break it out neatly at the top of a flagpole.

He learned the lines on Endeavour more quickly than anyone else I ever met.

'Knowing the ropes' is an essential if you want to be successful on Endeavour.

But he is completely incapacitated by sea-sickness. Last night, crouching for shelter in the lee of the capstan, his head in his hands, Bones was almost hallucinating.

"Poisonous shit," he said, when I offered him some tepid coffee with sugar in it. It was all I had.

Then: "my body's crying out for rest, it's telling me to sleep."

He lay down on the cold, wet deck as the boat heaved and shook towards the south. He passed out, comatose.

I looked for something to cover him, but there was nothing.

When I looked for him again, he had found his way off the deck, down below, into his hammock.

John Highmore is English, about 28. He was on the BBC voyage in 2001, so I know him well.

He speaks and writes Japanese and (I am told) performs a mean Japanese massage.

He is completely incapacitated by sea-sickness and he is the chef's only full-time assistant. I have been standing in for him all day, because he came into the galley this morning and had to leave in a rush before he threw up again.

I went to see him an hour ago, in his cabin. He had been lying, dreaming and dozing, in total darkness, for more than five hours. He had no idea of the time.

I gave him 2 dry biscuits, some water and an apple. I will take more water and biscuits to him later on.

It might take him three days or more to get back on his feet (though a few have managed to recover more promptly) and the symptoms may recur every time the ship hits rough weather on this or any future voyage.

*****

What it's like on board, especially when the weather is vile:

I have worked hard for twenty one of the last twenty seven hours. I should be on my knees.

1800-2000 on watch last night, 2330-0130 shortening sail, 0400-0730 on watch, 0730 to now (2130) in the galley.

I don't feel too bad on it. I had a forty minute nap this afternoon.

The boat is rolling fifty degrees to starboard, when it takes a big sea, and then another forty five degrees to port when it comes back.

As I write, there are clipboards hanging opposite me on a varnished, planked surface in the communal mess. I can estimate the angle of roll accurately by the swing of the clipboards, comparing it with the upright lines between the planks.

Ninety five degrees of roll is a lot.

It makes walking, working and cooking a nightmare.

In the galley, when I was preparing food, two onions escaped and rolled back and forth tantalisingly until I trapped them.

They hid under the furniture like rats, as if they had a life of their own.

We broke 2 plates and a mug.

With monotonous regularity, the dishes soon to be washed slid loudly onto the floor and clattered at our feet.

Everyone was very impressed with the food we turned out in these (trying) circumstances.

Bones managed to eat some of it.

Karl tried but failed. He only just made it out of the dining room without spewing.

Claire, who is about 20, nibbled dry biscuits instead of eating. She looked as they all do, glazed, sweaty and pale, looking into an inner darkness, into despair.

She is so small, so evidently young and so apparently vulnerable that she makes me feel very protective and sorry for her.

Seasickness is a terrible thing. And totally predictable and largely avoidable. If you have a good sense of balance, you will get sick at sea. If you take pills sufficiently far in advance, you will not be sick. You may be sleepy, spaced out and your judgement will be poor but you will not be sick. Take the pills before you leave the dock. It is by far the best option.

Take it from me, because I watch people suffer sea-sickness all the time and never suffer from it myself – I have no idea why. Perhaps I have a really bad sense of balance? Perhaps I would not be very good at walking a tight-rope? Who knows.

There are casualties. Already.

Bob, the Bob with a beard who resembles an animated gnome, missed his grip and fell on the back of his head. Seven stitches but evidently no concussion, no fracture of the skull – no after effects – Bob claims it's because he's thick, so his sense of humour hasn't deserted him even if his sense of balance has.

Tony, the guy who was severely sun-burned even before he came on board, fell and grazed his knee badly. Camilla seems to have cracked one or two of her ribs when she was thrown violently across the eighteenth century deck.

Shane seems to have done something nasty to himself but I am not sure what.

(Not the Shane from the BBC voyage who got deep vein thrombosis. A different Shane.)

It is wicked weather. The waves chase each other like boisterous schoolboys. They seem to shout a lot. Their play is rough and harsh – the white crests dancing with menace, like Muhammad Ali at his peak.

7/2 - Thursday

A very disturbed night. I didn't put my ear plugs in (I couldn't find them) and slinging my hammock in the dark, with all my shipmates comatose and close to me was endlessly difficult and unnerving.

The ship was still rolling wildly. It would have been easy to lose my balance and crash into one (or all) of them.

Then, when I got into the hammock, it sagged too low and snagged on a nearby cupboard.

I got out and slung it higher, Then I found myself bumping against Craig, to my left.

When I had adjusted it again, I was too wound up for sleep and thought about taking a sleeping pill – but I dozed off without one only for Jennaya to wake me for the midnight watch which I didn't have to stand because I had worked all day in the galley and was an honorary idler for the night. I thought again about the sleeping pill, but the next thing I knew it was morning and time to get up again, which I looked forward to. I can't think why.

Today, the seas have abated. The wild, angry beauty of the waves has faded into a dignified procession of quite orderly events. It is ten times easier to work and walk about.

It is nothing like as beautiful.

*****

8/2 - Friday

It has got so cold, so quickly.

Yesterday evening, we were only 300 miles SSW of Perth. which was sweltering. But the wind is howling at us out of the south or south east, from Antarctica. There is absolutely no refuge from it on deck, where we spend at least 8 hours of each day. It chills us to the bone. Normally, I would wear five, six or seven layers of warm clothes under my oilskins. But the set of oilies provided by Endeavour is too tight and small – not so much extra large as generous medium. I am not sure how to cope with this problem, which will get worse as we go further south.

At midnight, watch over, we creep to our hammocks.

Like the pale and sinister inhabitants of the lower world in H.G. Wells' 'The Time Machine', we scuttle half-bent under the bodies suspended, swaying, coccooned, in hammocks in the unstable gloom on the mess deck.

The ship rolls uneasily under power (and we have spent a lot of time under power since leaving Fremantle).

We are still trying to find the westerlies which will carry us quickly to Hobart. I sleep brilliantly, without pills, blindfolds or ear plugs, all of which I seem to have mislaid. I wake up happy and hurry to write all this down.

"Youth smiles without reason," wrote Oscar Wilde.

My young watch-mates certainly do. The girls are called Clare (whom I keep calling Kate) and Kate (whom I never call Clare). There is also a Claire on board (the one who was sea-sick) so it is all very confusing. Each of the three is, or appears to be, in her early twenties.

Amongst the young men on my watch are Alex, Craig and Bones.

Alex is great fun, boisterous and robust. He appeared very late and rather pink and flushed on the first night, Saturday, at dinner. (We were in a hostel. Endeavour was still in dry dock and miles away on the day we should have joined.)

He had failed to make contact with us, or with the ship, at the docks because the Endeavour Trust had failed to tell him which dock the ship would use and he had relied on sight of the ship's tall masts to track her down

When he had arrived, she was still far away, in dry dock, so this ploy was not successful and I think he had a very worrying afternoon trying to find out if the ship had somehow left without him and thinking that she had.

Since then, he has recovered his habitual high spirits and makes Craig and Bones laugh a lot, sometimes (when Craig is tired) almost hysterically.

Alex imitates gulls and gannets and there is a lot of mock pirate in his dialogue, as if he had watched the ship's favourite and, I think, only film (Blackbeard, with Robert Newton) once too often.

It sounds trite and childish, which it is, but I think we are all in a mood to be easily amused, today especially. The ship has stopped rolling, everyone is eating. The sun is shining, though the wind is bitter. We are heading, under power, in a direction where we ought to find some favourable wind.

Craig has sailed on Young Endeavour, a sail training ship, where Bones was on his watch. They know and like each other.

Craig has a long and amiable face, a high forehead, sleek hair and sideburns and looks a little older than the others. He worked in software design and used to make internet sites function.

I asked him why he was on Endeavour and he mimed pointing and clicking and pounding a keyboard.

"I'm here because of my shoulders," he said, hunching himself up as if stressed to distraction. He mimicked a scream of frustration. "I'm here to save my shoulders."

Watching Alex, Craig, Bones, Clare and Kate at the regular morning meeting, fooling around a little, smiling and laughing for no reason whatsoever, barracking the first officer, I admired three wonderful qualities which they share.

Insouciance, sociability and perfect teeth. What more could a young person want?

There is always a frivolous watch on a ship. One of the three watches is inevitably sillier than the others.

I am always - thank goodness - part of the silly watch. Sailing without laughter would not be the same at all.

Foremast watch at work

Tig and Andy caught a big tuna yesterday. It weighed more than 120 pounds. There was the usual noisy struggle to gaff it, secure it, lift it up the high sides of the ship. It was bleeding profusely. It was clearly dead or dying.

Andy and Tig held it up for the (many) cameras, thinking it was dead.

When they put it down, it came unexpectedly to life again, struggling desperately, tragically, for one last try at living.

Tig kicked it, hard, more than once. He had heavy boots on and he meant to hurt or kill it. The blood lust was on him.

I do not like to watch a living creature die but it is part of what happens if you fish for food. I have seen it before.

To kick a dying animal, of any type or species, is a horrible thing to do.

I was (and remain) revolted.

Yet I like Tig and I know him well enough to mention the kicking to him (I did the next day – he said, reasonably enough, that he wanted to hasten the fish's death, to stop it bruising itself in its last struggle. Why can I not quite accept that? Did I see something else in it, some aspect of a hidden streak of cruelty in him?)

Tig is Andy the shipwright's assistant now. as well as one of the keenest fishermen on board.

He was the boatswain's mate when I was on Endeavour last year.

Tig is about 27 years old, though I think he looks younger. He has a head of thick golden curls, which are his most distinctive feature.

Curiously, his curls make him look tougher rather than prettier.

Tig (from Tigger in the Pooh books – because he bounced around a lot when he was a child - his real name is Andrew) is square-built and robust, not very tall but probably very strong. He has a neat but piratical beard which is also golden in colour.

Andy is younger than Tig but taller and very strong and athletic. He has huge hands, the hands of a craftsman, which is what he is.

He was (I think) brought up in the country and he also has a game-keeper's skills and what I can only call long-distance eyes – as if he was about to scan a horizon or shoot at a game animal.

He is a very likeable, seemingly open, person, with a lot of natural authority, unusual in someone of only 24 years.

The fish was delicious. It fed more than fifty people at more than two meals.

The young women on board, especially those in the permanent crew, are, almost by definition, vigorous, athletic and independent. They wouldn't be here otherwise.

Lightly tanned, without make-up, climbing the rigging, they made me think of Betjeman's Miss Joan Hunter Dunn, 'furnished and burnished by Aldershot sun.'

On board, working, they seem to be without vanity.

On shore, no doubt, they transform themselves into glamour pusses, like caterpillars turning into butterflies.

They probably look just like everyone else.

10/2 - Sunday

3 minke whales blew and rushed towards us yesterday –
leaping and splashing back again – inquisitive and playful.
They were probably young ones – plumper and more
rounded (also smaller, c. 5m.) than the illustrations of
minke in the reference book I looked at.

We slowed down, and the engine note changed.

This seemed to worry them or discourage them. They
sounded when they were about 150 metres away, swam
underneath us and continued west at speed.

Quite a few albatross about yesterday, the slender wings
and huge wingspan very impressive.

Their aerodynamic profile reminds me of one of the USA's
heavy bombers and they use the wind and the uplifts and
thermals of the waves as if the atmosphere belonged to
them.

Which it does.

Black as velvet last night. No moon, no stars. Coming up
from the dim mess deck a little before 0400, the waist of the
ship is littered with obstacles and impenetrably invisible.
We are not allowed to use torches on deck.

You fumble your way to the first landmark (decking and
spars stowed at head height above the safety boat). You run
the fingers of your left hand along this until you can touch
a cannon with your right.

Just beyond the cannon are the steps up to the quarter
deck.

Your feet find them and you stumble up (holding on, all the
time holding on for dear life – the ship rolls without mercy,
all the time, even in moderate seas.)

At the top of the steps is another cannon, which you skirt cautiously, stepping over one of the mizzen staysail's preventers and under one of the same sail's sheets.

At this point, the outline of the lookout looms in the darkness. You mutter hello and stagger on. Sometimes you hear the reply and recognize the voice. More often, it is lost in the bitter-cold wind.

You stagger on towards the quarterdeck. If you are alert, you remember not to trip on the ropes from the helm.

If you take the helm, you are lucky because it gives you something to think about and you have to exert yourself.

Otherwise, you sit and shiver, on standby, in the darkness – no stars, no moon, no torchlight allowed (no reading), wondering why you came.

Sunday is a layday – we can leave our hammocks slung all day and do as little as possible.

But my watch has an unfortunate time with the rota on the first Sunday – we are on from midnight to four am, from noon to four pm and again from 8pm to midnight.

The lack of sleep is starting to affect me and I am a little irritable.

We are (at last) sailing in roughly the right direction but we don't need 12 people on deck to do so - I don't quite know why we spend so much time uncomfortably on standby on deck doing nothing.

Long chat with Claire, the girl who was so sea-sick. She will celebrate her 21st. birthday on passage (she didn't say when). She talked very openly, leafing through a scrapbook of sacred texts, photos of friends and love letters.

"I don't spend much time at home," she said, "my mum doesn't come home very much, my dad doesn't come home much. But I've got three families.

My Christian family – they kind of adopted me. And these guys too –" she showed me a picture. "So I've got lots of brothers and sisters and they're all between 18 and 22."

She paused at the picture of her VW Golf.

"My pride and joy," she said. "It's in the garage while I'm away. But my little sister gets her licence tomorrow, I think it's tomorrow. Is tomorrow the 11th?"

She thought about it.

"If her car breaks down, I guess mine gets to be the spare."

Her boy friend is called Callan. A letter to him was in the scrapbook and not hidden. It began "My darling Callan,"

I didn't have the time (or the gall) to read it.

Claire is gamine, with short cropped dark hair, bright brown eyes and cheeks as round as any apple. Her voice hasn't settled yet – it can be strident, almost harsh, curiously distinctive. She smiles all the time, as if concealing pain.

She has been christened Penguin, by her watch-mates, probably because she both squawks and flaps.

"I like you, you're funny," said someone to her.

"Well," she said – "if you can't laugh at yourself...."

Being sea sick so violently was difficult for her.

She was unforgettably grumpy one morning, when she was starting to get better.

She said later "if I could have killed someone, anyone, and got a dry patch of land to stand on, I would have killed someone this morning – that's how I felt, just anyone."

By accident, sometime later, I overheard a brief conversation about Claire in the mess. Two of her watch-mates talking ....

"What does she do?"

"I don't think she's come out into the real world yet."

A rather pompous comment, intended as a put-down.

But there might be a grain of truth in it.

The ashes of Ted and Audrey Mudge were scattered at sea yesterday. Gary told us a little bit about them. Audrey died first, three years ago, and expressed the wish that her ashes should be conjoined with Ted's. Ted had been an Endeavour Guide for many years, showing people round the ship when she is in port and functioning as a floating museum. He had also been in the Royal Navy and the Endeavour flew the Red Ensign at half mast at the stern in his honour, with the Australian flag (also at half mast) on the starboard flag halyard. The ship's bell tolled throughout the brief ceremony. There were no hymns or prayers. At Gary's request, I have hand-written a certificate for the relatives to record the occasion in my best calligraphic script, with a quill pen, on Endeavour's handsome headed paper.

It was a bit of a struggle, writing something like that on a ship wallowing in ocean waves - the inkpot kept trying to get away from me. I was terrified of the damp spoiling the script.

Also, how did Gary know I could write italic? I wouldn't have thought he had ever seen my handwriting and all my italic pens are back in London - curious.

Of course, on a small ship everyone gets to know almost everything about everybody pretty quickly - I suppose Martin or perhaps Sarah or John Highmore may have told him.

Anyway, it was fun to do. A distraction from the routine is always welcome.

How do these little girls learn so expertly to become young women? Kate is just 19, blonde, comely, athletic. She can climb a rope handily – she borrows crayons from Claire to colour in her diary/scrapbook. She is still both something of a tomboy and a little girl as well as a beautiful young woman.

Singing along with Bob Dylan and the Mamas and the Papas yesterday, sitting on the deck, how did she know to roll her eyes at just that moment, at just that angle, at the young man who was sitting opposite? Who taught her that? It could not have been more seductive.

Sadly, it was not meant for me to see. Most certainly not.

Her father is on board, and I am even older than he is.

One Foot in the Grave? Like the great Richard Wilson?

Not quite.

But it might look that way to a nineteen year old.

*****

11/2 - Monday around midnight

I am beginning to understand why the Ancient Mariner thought the Southern Ocean was haunted.

It changes uncannily quickly and unexpectedly.

You never know what's going to happen next with the weather.

At lunchtime, after a galloping run yesterday (160 nautical miles noon to noon), we were still sailing in 20-23 knots of ENE breeze.

But the ship was pressed, over-canvassed.

The wind was gusting up to 28 or more knots so we reefed the topsails (20+ bodies – it took about an hour) and re-hoisted the sails.

The ship sailed flatter, seemed more comfortable. The rolling motion settled. We were still making more than six knots.

By this evening, the picture had changed completely. The wind backed from the east to the north. It gusted irritably, as if it could start up towards a gale or die completely.

The waves were tall and angry, perhaps 12-15 feet from trough to peak. It rained hard and our oilskins leaked miserably.

Then, suddenly, a cold front overtook us. The rain stopped, the seas were still, the wind died down.

Mist flooded towards us from the distant horizons, soon totally obscured.

Silence overwhelmed us like a blanket. The ship drifted forwards, powered by its own momentum and a favourable current. No one spoke on deck. It was very sudden and mysterious. It felt ominous.

We took in sail and squared the yards. We ran about like banshees. Everyone who was anybody shouted.

But the big squall we feared never came. Our average speed declined to zero. When my watch came down, at midnight, all the sails were still half-trimmed, half-braced, waiting for a wind that never came.

13/2 - Wednesday – 0500

Snatched a few hours sleep, then back on watch. Writing this in my coffee break (and my favourite pen is failing). Fortunately, I have another, similar.

We are under power again, heading east, which probably means we have given up the drive south to find the wind.

I think we may have managed the worst of all possible worlds - chasing south to find the westerlies, not finding them and positioning ourselves accidentally just between two highs, going too fast for the one behind us to catch up, too slowly to catch the one ahead.

Certainly the sea is calm, there is no wind at all. Pillars of cloud reach up to the sky in the east as the dawn creeps up on us.

Mars is the last Heavenly body to fade back into the sky.

Worth remembering how remote this area is – and we are only 8-900 miles south of Australia.

We haven't seen a vessel or an aeroplane since we left Fremantle (which the kids call Freo) 8 days ago.

We calculate that it would take a naval vessel at least 2-3 days to reach us if we had a medical emergency.

The First Officer on this trip is Glen Hope, who has known Endeavour and all on board her for many years. I think he helped to build her.

He is very efficient indeed, with a vaguely military moustache and a leather belt with rather too many buckles on it.

I think he feels that Endeavour has gone to the dogs since his time and that he is just the man to revitalize the ship, re-organize her and raise the level of maintenance and administration.

All First Officers probably feel like that, about almost every ship which they join or re-join.

Certainly Gordon, the First Officer on the BBC voyage, was remarkably laid back by comparison with Glen. But then he did not have the responsibility of setting off for a long, long journey and pulling together a completely new ship's company to sail a unique and uniquely obsolete ship round Cape Horn. And Glen joined the ship at very short notice, when Gordon left quite suddenly.

Glen laughs a lot, but not always with his eyes. He has a very quick wit and a surprisingly elaborate wardrobe and, at the morning meetings, he puts up with a lot of lip from the assembled youngsters, especially about what he wears. His knowledge of old ships and the techniques for sailing them and for maintaining them are very impressive. He is an expert sail-maker.

Also on board, for the first leg, to Hobart, is an extra Captain, Captain Dai – a small garrulous Welshman with a fund of sea-stories and bombast.

Dai is as warm as the coal fire on my canal boat on a winter's night. A lovely man.

He has used the Marq Saint-Hilaire method of calculating position lines and what I call 'the horrible Haversines' for the whole of his life and will have no truck with scientific calculators and the like.

He showed me his navigational notebooks, dating back to his very earliest voyages and they are a model of neatness and precision which make me ashamed of the muddles that I perpetrate when working by hand.

Very old school. Very splendid. Very effective.

Later:

Gorgeous day's sailing – dropped the reefs and hauled topsails immediately after morning meeting – about 6.75 knots at 100 degrees magnetic ever since.

14/2 - Thursday – 0720

The cold has taken on another dimension. Within the first few days of the passage, the wind from the south turned bitter chill. Since then, with winds from the north and north east, it has not been too bad on night watch.

This morning's middle watch, twelve midnight till 0400, was seriously cold. I wore five out of a total possible seven, layers of clothing and still felt it.

Later, in my hammock, in a sleeping bag, on a mattress, wearing a T shirt and underpants, I was frozen.

I think the cold woke me early, to give me the time to get up and write all this down.

Certainly, there is no time to spare except these manufactured moments, stolen from the routine.

The watches follow each other ruthlessly, suddenly, irregularly interspersed with cleaning details, stints of maintenance work on the ship, the meals and a few hours of blessed sleep.

The days are hard – almost harsh – in their repetitive intensity.

Bones, in particular, is exhausted. He tells me he normally sleeps 9-10 hours each night, so a few scratched, scattered and interrupted hours in a hammock, built around the disruptive middle watch, are little use to him.

His eyes are huge, his face pale and strained, he mumbles rather than speaks and sometimes what he says makes little sense.

This morning, he looks a bit better although he is still obviously exhausted.

But a day like yesterday, sunshine on white bright waves, the ship driving powerfully forward, hour after hour, day after day, inexhaustibly, will make all of us well and fresh again.

The sea is a great doctor, sailing a great tonic. The daily struggle, for sleep, leisure, warmth, is something we have to accept in return.

*****

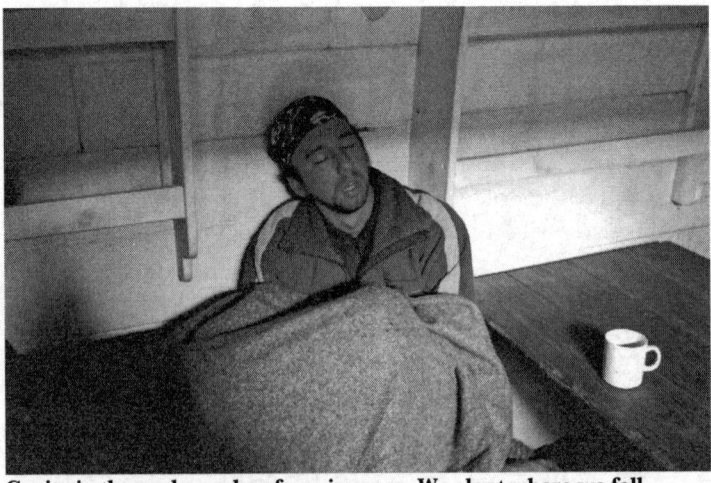

Craig, in the early weeks of our journey. We slept where we fell.

14/2 - Thursday (continued)

I had forgotten this was St. Valentine's Day and also the anniversary of Captain Cook's death.

On this day, in 1779, the Hawaians stoned and mobbed him, killed him and ate him.

Only a few of his bones were ever recovered. (Were there reprisals? What did his crew do afterwards? There is nothing in my edition of Cook's Journals to clarify this point. I must look it up elsewhere when I reach shore.)

There were reprisals. Stephen Bown writes in "An Age of Scurvy" as follows: "The English mariners, unrestrained by Cook's stern authority, went on a bloodthirsty, revenge-fuelled rampage, shooting islanders and burning their village. Dozens were killed before the Resolution and the Adventure finally departed."

At the morning meeting, Malcolm Hay read an account of Cook's death and Endeavour flew the Red Ensign, at half mast, in honour of the event.

This solemnity was replaced by farce later in the day when the First Officer ordered a number of the men into female costume so that there would be a 'date' for everyone on board to romance at dinner.

The results were gruesome in the extreme.

Kevin's heavily bearded leer, his mini-skirt and his thigh length woolen stockings were unforgettable and Lawrence, who is very young and thin, with curly black hair and very red lips, joined in rather too enthusiastically, shaving his legs and side burns and affecting an alarmingly girlish falsetto.

"You can't handle a real woman," he lisped when John H. remonstrated.

John was not impressed.

After dinner, a cold front hit us.

At first it was mysterious and quiet. The sea mist encircled us like a regiment of ghosts.

The seas flattened, the wind whispered. Then the rain came suddenly – it was torrential, piercing rain with gusts of wind up to 40 knots.

The ship rolled and pitched horribly as we climbed the foremast and out onto the yard to furl the topsail.

When we were down again, we went up the main mast to furl the mainsail, the main course.

The wet, heavy canvas blew up in our faces and the gaskets, the lines to tie the sail up to the yard, blew away from us as we tried with numb fingers, blinded by the rain, in almost total darkness, to make things tidy.

I have totally under-estimated the violent potential of the weather on this journey.

Tonight is only another beginning. It will get worse than this, much worse, much much worse.

I can cope with the discomfort, the exertions, the elements of danger, but not with soaking wet feet and water running down my chest under my clothes while standing, waiting interminably, for 4-5 hours without a break, for the next command, in 40 knots of wind. That makes me miserable.

In Hobart, I will spend whatever it costs to re-equip myself. I hope the chandler has been warned to anticipate increased demand for warm clothing, thermal underwear and sea boots. Otherwise, he will run out.

Every day, every night, after the watch, when I generally feel exhausted, I examine myself in the mirror as I clean my teeth.

I expect to look haggard, pale and drawn. Instead, I look tanned, well-fed and extremely satisfied with my lot (albeit dishevelled).

I smile a lot on board a sailing ship – even when things are tough.

15/2 - Friday

This morning, the weather has been even worse but at least it's been exciting and we are making rapid progress, in something like the right direction. A front came through quite early and brought with it the usual heavy rain but also winds up to 60 knots and mountainous seas. The wind backed 110 degrees in just a few minutes.

All the sails except one (the foremast course) had to be handed and furled promptly, which we managed quite quickly and the ship ploughed on through great bright seas, shining with sunlight, with the foam blowing beautifully off the front of the big fierce breaking waves just like Admiral Beaufort said it would when he was categorising the size of seas and the strength of winds and the way that waves would look to compile the Beaufort scale in the middle of the nineteenth century.

Endeavour was running away from the storm as if her life depended on it (which it did), the wind roaring in the rigging and the boat rolling nearly 100 degrees from side to side and three of the strongest people in the watch were struggling to control the wheel and to follow Captain Dai's peremptory and authoritative instructions:

Five Spokes to Port

Midships

Three Spokes to Port

Two Spokes to Starboard

... all without expression, fear or emotion. He was watching the waters and the waves behind us, calculating the swing of the ship by the second.

It was heavy work on the helm and I was exhausted after 40 minutes. I can still feel it, hours later, in my left shoulder, in the muscles of my arms.

Captain Dai did well that day. I think he was on deck continuously for nine hours.

Will Studd, Kate's father, an expert on cheese, stayed on the helm for more than an hour and Stuart the gold-miner did the same. They are both exceptionally fit and strong.

Nigel Longster, a New Zealander with a weakness for beards, tattoos, Harley Davidsons and bull terriers, assisted them for most of that time. They were enjoying it too, the three of them, till Nigel was called away for his regular stint of galley duty, which must have been fairly ghastly in those conditions.

Between decks, when it is really rough, the ship creaks and groans as if she were distressed or injured.

In the galley, however you arrange it, the pots and pans clank and jingle and something noisy, like an empty baking tin or a tin mug, escapes and clatters back and forth across the floor.

We nearly broached just once when I was on deck, when we got a bit sideways to the waves. We started to broach up and stalled and the forecourse backed and the helm was not answering.

Hard to Port, said Dai

and then, loudly

All the way over

Dai was suddenly very watchful as he waited for the helm to answer. Gary looked a little tense, as he has all morning.

She came back. The ship found herself again. These waves would be big enough to knock her down and dismast her if we steered her badly.

Bob was hit by a rope and has opened up the stitches in his skull. The other Bob is seasick again. I am told that we averaged more than 8.5 knots for the whole of the morning.

16/2 - Saturday

Very tired. The motion of the ship is still extreme though the wind is below 30 knots. The struggle not to hurt yourself as you move around is an uneven one. It is a losing battle, trying to be comfortable.

We went on deck at 0400, dry, well-equipped, ready for our watch. Before we had even numbered off and taken over the helm, a huge wave swept over the quarter deck, which has been dry so far on this voyage.

The wave went over my head as I sat, pulling on my gloves. I licked salt from my lips and cheeks after it passed.

It completely soaked my feet and my clean, dry socks.

Fortunately, I was well braced. It didn't carry me away.

Jon Preston was less fortunate. He was not clipped on and it swept him (and another guy) into the scuppers. He thought he was going over the side.

To go over my head, the wave must have been about five foot deep on the quarterdeck.

The quarterdeck (in flat water) is more than fifteen feet from the surface of the sea. That makes the wave twenty to twenty five feet in height, travelling at 90 degrees to our direction and to the direction of the wind and all the other waves.

Later, with soggy wet feet and shoes, I tried to hurry back on deck.

The ship rolled unexpectedly and I bashed my ankle and my left toe, badly.

Later still, helping in the galley, I again tried to hurry and cut myself.

Later yet, I discovered a nasty bruise on my hip (though I cannot remember where or when I received it). I have been quite manic today.

I am over-tired and I can't relax. I want to put my arms around somebody - anybody - and hug really hard.

17/2 - Sunday

Lay day – transcribing journal onto Martin's computer, so no time to write more.

Good speed. Great skies at night. Yesterday's big wave flooded the eighteenth century deck and the twentieth century mess deck below it – there was a lot of mopping up which I didn't know about.

Marcia, one of the supernumeraries, was woken by the commotion, sat up hurriedly, and now has her head in a big bandage – she cut it open on a low flying shelf of some sort.

Due in Hobart 1000 on Tuesday, which is not bad given that we left a day late.

18/2 - Monday

Arrival time postponed till Tuesday afternoon – I missed observing the MerPass (the Meridional Passage of the sun, aka the noon shot) – I was just too busy, cleaning, taking part in a line race, handing sails, having late lunch.

We lost the line race by one point because our distinguished watchmate, Malcolm Hay, the former orthopaedic surgeon, tried to nobble the opposition and got found out.

Our team was fined two points and that made the fatal difference.

19/2 - Tuesday

Up at 0700, did my routine stint in the galley washing the breakfast dishes, then up on deck watching the unspoiled and very pretty coast of Tasmania slide by.

We passed Little Oyster cove, Bligh point, the Derwent river.

What very evocative names there are round here .....

A morning meeting, as usual, with all the voyage crew, then a special meeting in the Great Cabin, for the 14 stalwarts who are sailing all the way to Whitby.

Eight of them are in my watch. Of the men, only Jon and I are not sporting a beard.

At lunchtime, we dropped four people who were in a hurry to get ashore (Will Studd amongst them - I was sorry to see him go).

Our Rigid Inflatable (RIB - aka, 'the fizz boat') took them in to Dover, a fishing port sheltering cleverly behind a lush green island off the wonderfully named d'Entrecasteaux Channel.

The sun was shining, the wind dead set against us but mild and pleasant, driving the spray over the bows and back to the quarter deck where it fogged my spectacles so much I had to take them off.

We will be in Hobart by this evening and then the first leg of the journey will be over for ever.

I am not sure I am ready for that.

*****

Hobart - Endeavour alongside

Great place for a picnic

SHIPMATES

Endeavour would just be a shell, a floating museum, without a crew to work her. The people who work on Endeavour and who make Endeavour work are very intriguing and often very different, from each other and from whatever counts for 'normal' in our complicated on-shore world. They are the people who make Endeavour come alive.

There are several different categories of people on board.

First, the members of the professional crew, led by the deck officers, like Glen Hope and Sarah Robinson and the navigators and warrant officers Gerald Collins, Dougal Herd, the boatswain, and Andy Law, the shipwright.

Then come the supernumeraries, who often join in and help with the ship's work (but do not have to). They pay extra for their passages and occupy cabins in the stern, below the quarterdeck, where the officers and the gentlemen lived in Cook's time. They have the use of the wardroom and access to the Great Cabin and they see the Captain occasionally for drinks and suppers and sometimes (very English) afternoon tea.

Supernumeraries have the privilege of leisure, if they want it.

Finally, the voyage crew who pay to sail this unique and demanding ship and who come on board knowing that they may have to turn out at night to haul the halyards or the sheets or brace the yards, that they must follow any reasonable order while they are on board, and that they will have to climb 100 feet up the masts even if the sea is rough and the wind is blowing hard, even if the ratlines and shrouds are covered in ice and it is snowing.

They work or stand watch for up to 16 hours per day six days per week and up to at least eight hours per day on the seventh.

The voyage crew sleep in hammocks on the communal eighteenth century deck where their lives are distinguished by an absolute lack of privacy, frequent sleep deprivation, limited natural light, an absence of ventilation and salt water running down from the bulkheads on top of them as they try to sleep.

They have a lot of fun.

"We've just laughed all the way across the Pacific," said Pete the Fish (Peter Deakin) when we eventually arrived at Cape Horn.

Pete was 58 years old at that time and he had joined the ship at Hobart to sail all the way to Britain. He lived in New Zealand, he was a professional fisherman and mariner, and he still had relations in Bridlington (Yorkshire) and near Flamborough Head.

But he looked very drawn and very cold when we came off watch one night at four in the morning.

"I thought this trip would rejuvenate me," he said mournfully. "But I think I'll get off this ship on crutches."

Voyage crew mostly dress in rags (but then so do the professional crew and any sensible supernumeraries.) Any clothes that are not rags when you begin a trip on Endeavour are soon made into rags as the journey progresses. Endeavour, like any eighteenth century ship where the standing rigging is made of natural fibres and preserved with tar, is not a place for smart clothes or genteel affectations.

The people on board co-exist in cramped, damp spaces in a tiny wooden ship and look out every morning (as Pepys noted) on the infinite grandeur of the world's oceans and the infinite beauty of the sky.

Every evening they can marvel at the majesty of the stars and the planets. Their minds roam free. Only the wind and the waves matter. And getting enough food and sleep.

The Greeks thought that sailors ranked somewhere between the living and the dead, belonging neither to the earth nor to the heavens.

The people who work Endeavour have all been touched by the magic or the madness of the sea and the beauty of the ship. They are infected by it.

Some of them return time and again, to try to purge the infection and free themselves, muttering each time, as they disembark, that they will never come back, that this time is the last. But the wind whispers to them on the quayside and the gulls hymn them as they lug their bags ashore and their mind fills with the possibility of adventure soon again and against their will, as if pulling them along, something inside them inspires and possesses them:

"Just one more time," they say, "just one more time."

*****

MODESTY, ABLUTIONS AND DIET

On Cook's Endeavour, there were no women. Modesty was not an issue and there were un-shielded urinals on deck (just as there are on the replica) and two 'seats of ease' in the bows from which the all-male crew could defecate directly into the sea. Something similar, for the use of the officers, would have been provided in the stern.

These 'seats of ease' in the bows are unshielded on the replica, though I have my doubts whether Joseph Banks and his gentleman-scientist colleagues would have wanted to watch the numerous Endeavour crew members drop their britches every day for two or three years without a screen or some improvised equivalent to provide a modicum of privacy.

They would also have been unusable in anything like rough weather.

On the BBC voyage in 2001, we were not forced to use the 'seats of ease' but went to the lavatories below the waterline where there were also hot showers, wash basins and washing machines.

We did not use these twentieth century washing facilities at all on the BBC voyage, though I once caught one of the girls washing her hair down there - she had long, long hair and she said that washing it in salt water with salt water soap was messing it up enormously.

I can believe it. I washed in salt water on deck for the six weeks of that first voyage and, thinking it unnecessary, I rarely rinsed myself off in the fresh water that was provided.

As a result, I got salt water sores by the time we were back on shore. I didn't recognize them as such and was concerned in case the diet or some other factors were responsible.

Fortunately, the young doctor, Claire, set me straight. Apparently the salt in salt water can block the pores and the result is a little like a sebaceous cist - quite painful and very obvious but not at all threatening.

When I told this story to a group of young Australians, I was met with complete indignation and disbelief. "I never shower after I go the beach!" said one. "It just ain't true!" said another.

But I can't imagine Captain Cook's crew ever having fresh water to rinse themselves down after a soaking or if they washed their bodies. I bet they had salt water sores. And where would they have washed in bad weather when the hold of Cook's Endeavour, now the area where the toilets and showers are found, was packed with provisions and gunpowder and (eventually) botanical specimens and research materials. And how on earth did they wash their clothes?

These are some of the issues that I was still thinking about two years after Endeavour disgorged the BBC gang into the fleshpots of Bali for a memorable but largely unremembered end-of-voyage party. Our watchleaders mooned us as we departed. I am afraid the professional crew on Endeavour found the skittish vitality of the BBC gang more than a little annoying. But I loved them dearly. They were very entertaining and inquisitive. We put up with each other and with a very inadequate simulation of an eighteenth century diet without too many complaints - except about the washing facilities. The lack of clean shirts was a privation too far for that lot.

I wrote to them all when I had had time to do some research:

> For reasons of my own, and just for fun, I have been looking into the living conditions of eighteenth century sailors and the ways that the ships of that time were manned and managed.
> Remembering the pretend eighteenth century food that we were given, I thought it might interest you all to know the exact dietary allowances of the time, which were as follows:
>
> 1lb. bread per day, 1 gallon beer per day (or the equivalent in rum, wine or brandy), 4lbs. beef and 2 lbs. pork per week, 2 pints of peese (peas), 3 pints oatmeal, 6 ozs. butter, 12 ozs. cheese.
>
> There was also 'portable soup', a dried concoction something like a stock cube, which could be re-hydrated. There's a recipe for it in a wonderful book called Lobscouse and Spotted Dog, (p. 241).
>
> Of course, 'bread' here means ship's biscuits, which, as we all found out, are incredibly and inedibly hard until the weevils get at them and they become "like calves' foot jelly or blancmange," as one contemporary wrote.
>
> On Christopher Colombus's fourth voyage, his son wrote graphically about conditions on board. A great book by Reay Tannahill, 'Food in History' records this remark:
>
> "And what with the heat and the dampness, even the biscuit was so full of worms that, God help me, I saw many wait until

nightfall to eat the porridge made of it so as not to see the worms."

But, writes the celebrated naval historian, N.A.M. Rodger, "by the standards of the poor, naval food was good and plentiful."

Puddings (duffs) and porridges were the mainstay:

"Monday was cheese and duff, Tuesday boiled beef, Wednesday peas and duff, Thursday boiled pork, Fridays peas and duff, Saturday boiled beef, Sunday boiled pork and a treat such as figgy dowdy," which was ship's biscuit with bacon, fruit and gravy.

Doesn't sound too bad, does it?

Captain Cook was also, as we know to our cost, charged by the Admiralty with making "a fair tryal ..... of the efficacy of the Sour Kraut against the Scurvy" and, like Captain Chris Blake, was obsessive about cleanliness and its connection with the health of his men.

"Filthiness (is) a chief source of infection and cleanliness an excellent preservative," wrote one of Cook's contemporaries and new recruits were compelled to be washed, de-loused and re-clothed when they joined a ship.

In 1747, James Lind was investigating scurvy and general health amongst seamen and wrote: "the number of seamen in times of war who die of shipwreck, capture, famine, fire or sword, are but inconsiderable in respect of such as are destroyed by the ship's diseases."

This can also be true even in the modern period.

"One outbreak of viral gastroenteritis on a naval vessel in 1997 affected 1,807 crew members, 43% of the ship's company," reported the Guardian newspaper on 4th. November, 2003.

So Captain Blake's emphasis on us all spending time cleaning the ship every blessed morning was a sensible precaution even if, on some occasions, many hands seemed to make not for light work but for inefficiency and inadvertent obstructiveness and carelessness.

The average eighteenth century seaman was 22-24 years old, with seven years experience, and found the Navy a good life. One of them remembered that he "thought of nothing but pleasant gales and prosperous voyages." There were dangers, certainly, but an Able Seaman could earn about £14 per year at a time when a ploughman earned £3.

Shipmates wanted to stick together and the ties of loyalty went between shipmates and between the men and their officers. "Good followers were the foundation of an officer's success," writes N.A.M. Rodger.

A group of seamen wished to follow a good officer to another ship.

So they loyally petitioned the officer himself and the Port Admiral to be allowed to do so and their petition has survived. The spelling is interesting because it shows clearly the level of literacy amongst them. They obviously had little to do with the written word and little formal education.

"If your honer would be Cind A Nuf to Right to the Lords of the Admirlte ... We All Would be glad to go A Long with your honer A gain."

There are some lovely books about all this. I have quoted from NAM Rodger's The Wooden World (1986) and from Blake and Lawrence's Nelson's Navy (2000) as well as the others mentioned.

History came alive when we went on Endeavour and it remains a very lively and enlightening experience when I look back on it. I am sure some of you feel much the same.

All the best to all of you, as always, and it's good to hear your Nues when you can be Bovered to Right ...

Hygiene and nutrition were subjects close to Captain Cook's heart. His Endeavour had no galley as such - cooking was done on the big stove on the Eighteenth Century deck, food preparation (I assume) on deck or on the tables in the same area. It is difficult to visualize - barrels of salt pork or beef hoisted up from the holds below the waterline, forced open and then - with no clean fresh water to steep them and soak them - the highly salt meats cooked off without onions, garlic or fresh vegetables to make them palatable. It is not a recipe or a prospect that attracts me.

How did this diet keep the men alive, when men who are active at sea need more than 3,000 calories per day to retain their body weight?

The quantities that Cook stored on board Endeavour were absolutely huge and the daily allowances (as noted above) were very generous indeed. Simon Baker includes the following quotation in his book 'The Ship'.

Victualling Board Minutes 15 June, 1768

"Let the following provisions be sent to the said Bark (Endeavour) as desired, viz: Bread in Bags 21,226 pounds. Ditto in butts 13,440 pounds, flour for Bread in Barrels 9,000 pounds. Beer in Puncheons 1,200 gallons. Spirits 1,600 gallons. Beef 4,000 pieces. Flour in lieu of ditto in half barrels 1,400 pounds. Suet 800 pounds. Raisins 2,500 pounds. Peas in butts 187 bushels. Oatmeal 10 ditto. Wheat 120 bushels. Oil 120 gallons. Sugar 1,500 pounds. Vinegar 500 gallons. Sauerkraut 7,860 pounds. Malt in hogsheads 40 bushels. Salt 20 ditto. Pork 6,000 pieces. Mustard seed 160 pounds."

At 1lb. per head, per man, the bread or biscuits laden would have been sufficient for more than 430 days at sea. This accords well with what Cook thought himself about the provisioning.

From the Journals:

26th. August, 1768: "At 2pm got under sail and put to sea, having on board 94 persons including officers, seamen, gentlemen and their servants, near 18 months provisions, 10 carriage guns, 12 swivels with good store of ammunition and stores of all kinds."

Also on board, dozens of chickens, some sheep, a goat, a pig, a sow and their piglets. No bullocks? Perhaps there was just not enough room

Perhaps none were available and Cook was relying on acquiring some animals and slaughtering and salting them down when he called at ports on his route.

Another thing that is surprising is the quantity of alcohol.

"It seems remarkable," writes N.A.M. Rodger, "that officers managed, on the whole, to stay sober when they had to be, except perhaps that the prospect of drowning concentrates a man's mind wonderfully."

The men did not stay sober.

A drunken night-time brawl saw the Captain's Clerk lose the clothes off his back and bits of his ears as well and, on another occasion, the Gunner (with two others) "found means to take out of the spirit cask on the quarter deck between 10 and 12 gallons of rum .... they were caught in the act and ... punished with 12 lashes each," which was the maximum punishment that a Captain could inflict without breaking Admiralty regulations.

The Endeavour, on departure, must have been over-crowded, over-laden and awe-inspiringly packed to the gunwales with booze, provisions, equipment, animals and people.

No wonder the Admiralty preferred a converted cargo vessel to a warship for the expedition. And the Endeavour, with its shallow draft and flat bottom, could take the ground, to be careened (tipped on her side) and repaired out of range of a dockyard if necessary - as she was after she ran up on to the Great Barrier Reef on 11th. June, 1770.

Why sauerkraut (or Sour Kraut)? How would sauerkraut keep men in good health, when scurvy was still a killer? Also, at 2lbs per man per week, Cook only had enough sauerkraut for about 40 weeks. Was he relying on obtaining other substances to supplement it? How good was Cook at looking after his men, especially on the first of his voyages?

The health record of Cook's voyages has become a matter of some dispute. In his reports to the Admiralty and his journals (which were also submitted to the Admiralty), he seems to have over-emphasized or exaggerated how well his men coped with the extreme privations of his very long voyages.

Joseph Banks, in his own unofficial journal of the first voyage, reports exhaustion and what he calls 'Nostalgia', a crippling form of lethargy and disinterest which is almost certainly symptomatic of incipient scurvy and which (he claims) afflicted the whole crew after they left the east coast of Australia where they had regularly been able to obtain fresh meat and vegetables.

Even before that, "the People began to be very Sickeley," as he wrote on 11th. October, 1769, when Endeavour was still circumnavigating New Zealand.

Banks recalls the beautiful green of the island of Timor, where Cook would not stop, and then the diseased atmosphere of Batavia (Jakarta) with "mosquitoes breeding in every splash of water."

Whether Banks knew or suspected that mosquitoes were disease carriers is unclear, but malaria and dysentery picked up in Batavia did for 26 of Cook's crew as they started to traverse the Indian Ocean and sail home round the Cape of Good Hope and others also died variously from drowning, consumption, alcohol or epilepsy.

"It was not an impressive health record," write R. Fisher and H. Johnston in Captain Cook and his Times (1979) where they also reprint "Medical Aspects and Consequences of Cook's Voyages" by Sir James Watt, which analyses Cook's second and third voyages in detailed medical terms.

I disagree completely with Fisher and Johnston. Only 33 men died of disease on Cook's first great voyage of discovery. Two others froze to death, three drowned, one deserted. One was discharged. A man was pressed in Mauritius. The numbers are confusing but a full crew list is at the end of this book.

If Cook brought back 55 men in good health after three years at sea, it was a triumph. It was not unusual for 70-90% of a crew to die on passage at that time, or for great warships to be left without enough crew to sail them and manage the guns at the same time. Also, it seems that none of Cook's crew died of the scurvy during the first voyage and there was certainly no reason for them to do so, even without sauerkraut in their diet.

By the time of Cook's voyage, quite a lot was known about scurvy - much more than we sometimes imagine.

Its symptoms were swelling of the gums, denting of the flesh and lethargy leading eventually to death - just the symptoms which Joseph Banks recorded amongst Cook's crew after the Endeavour rounded Cape York and set sail for what were then called 'The Dutch East Indies'.

Very early on, in the medieval period, the Chinese knew to ward off scurvy by growing ginger on board their big ships on passage and the Dutch seem to have learned from them that greenstuff and fruit juice were crucial dietary supplements for long-distance sailors.

The English East India Company dispatched its first ships to the Indies in 1601 and they hove to off the southern tip of Madagascar and gathered "oranges and lemons of which we made good store ... which is the best remedy against scurvy."

But, even 150 years later, this was still regarded as too expensive a solution for naval use and conventional medical opinion dogmatically held that established and practical nautical solutions (dosing the men with lemon juice, making them eat fresh vegetables) could not possible do away with a 'disease' like scurvy.

Stephen R. Bown in 'The Age of Scurvy' (2005) makes it clear that medical professionals regarded scurvy as a disease and not as a nutritional deficiency until almost the end of the eighteenth century, which was a crucial mistake.

Only in 1794 did the Admiralty start to insist on mixing lemon juice with the rum ration throughout the fleet, "to the tune of 1.6 million gallons ... between 1795 and 1815. The mortality rate showed a gratifyingly steep decline," as Reay Tannahill writes in 'Food in History'.

Admiral Vernon , in Jamaica, started to mix lemon juice with the rum ration of the West Indies fleet in 1740 and used it to replace brandy, which had previously been the official spirit offered.

Did nobody notice that scurvy disappeared as a result? Or look carefully at Dr. James Lind's masterful and exhaustive "Treatise of the Scurvy," published in 1753.

By the middle of the nineteenth century, lime juice from the west Indies (though much less generously packed with Vitamin C than lemon or orange juice) had begun to be standard British naval issue, mixed with the rum. The myth of the 'limey' sailors and their peculiar dietary habits had started to take root. Most other navies stuck to lemon or orange juice until the advent of vitamin pills in the twentieth century. But of course lime juice was cheaper and the British Admiralty is nothing if not parsimonious. Men's lives were very cheap when Captain Cook set off on passage.

When I worked for a few days in the galley on Endeavour the weather was desperately rough and John Highmore was desperately seasick. It was appalling, quite shocking, to encounter such foul weather so soon. We were just a few hundred miles from Fremantle. We had half the planet still to navigate.

As I was chopping up ten or twelve large onions, the stainless steel vessels hanging on the bulkheads clattered and the stainless steel ladles and spoons clanged loudly against each other - the noise was terrific.

Meanwhile, anything you couldn't tie down would escape from the chopping board and rush, with the roll of the ship, into the corners of the large modern galley, beneath the waterline of this impeccable eighteenth century reconstruction.

Endeavour feeds its crew of 56 people very well - they need it. It is plain food, without pretensions, but it definitely hits the spot, especially when the formidable Jo Mannington is in charge.

Jo is a New Zealander, a stalwart of the Endeavour family. She came back to the ship, at very very short notice, on the Cape Horn voyage, to take charge of the catering.

They all come back.

The crew get off the ship after a long passage, breathe sighs of relief, kiss the ground and embrace their family and friends.

Six months later, they are back on board listening to all the safety lectures again and being told (again and again) how to use the grey valves in the lavatories and how best to don life jackets and wriggle into immersion suits.

Jo is the same.

I do not know how many miles she has sailed on the Endeavour but I doubt that anyone except the Captain has sailed further. She has certainly done most of the Pacific, twice, all of the Atlantic and round Cape Horn.

Jo is a charismatic woman, then in her thirties, who runs the Endeavour galley with great expertise and authority and turns out lots of extremely good grub with an apparent lack of effort which defies nature. Fresh bread is baked each day and pizzas and good salads are baked, mixed, constructed, adroitly served and consumed all in the same area.

I once owned a restaurant and I think I know something about catering for and feeding large numbers, but Jo is something else.

Even in the worst of the weather, she was always on top of the whole problem of running the galley and turning out 150 good meals a day in huge seas with just one (seasick) assistant.

I only worked in Endeavour's galley before Jo came on board. She didn't need emergency help at any time.

That was when the quartet of onions got away from me.

Have you ever chased an onion round a kitchen on a ship rolling heavily and pitching like a corkscrew?

Have you ever pursued a tin of tomatoes under a galley cupboard?

These inanimate objects seem to take on a life of their own as the waves propel them from corner to corner - they're like rats, defying you to catch them.

It didn't half make me laugh.

*****

21st. February, 2002 - Thursday

Email from Hobart to my former shipmates, the BBC gang, who were with me on Endeavour in 2001.

Hello again and thank you for all your e-mails and good wishes. Please forgive me for not replying individually - time is always short even in port when we are supposedly free of our usual watch keeping duties. In practice, there is always something that we ought to be doing for Endeavour. She thrives on attention, like a spoiled child or a temperamental vintage motor car.

We plan to leave Hobart tomorrow for Bluff, in New Zealand, where we call before we cross the Pacific and round the Horn. It'd be good to hear from you all in Rio about 28th. April. That will be probably be the next time I surface.

I am longing to be away and rather anxious about it simultaneously. It is a long way to go and a long time to be without the comforts and benefits of civilization - personal freedom, privacy, cleanliness and alcohol are amongst the things I most miss.

It is also very unsettling to be wafting round Hobart all day shopping for heavy oilskins and thick, warm socks and then to return to Endeavour in the evenings to try to sleep. A big wooden sailing ship in harbour is always a desperate place, confused, noisy, dirty, without the routine it needs to sustain it. Hobart has been great fun - lots of partying and very little sleep. The bar-tenders will miss us even if no one else does.

The new people who have joined here are good too - most of them very experienced sailors, probably 80-90% on their second or third voyage on board Endeavour. Well, we will need experienced hands where we are going. The taste of heavy weather we had while on the way from Fremantle was pretty convincing. If it is going to get any worse than that (and I think it is) we will be struggling.

But I am enjoying it hugely – great companionship, amazing sailing,and this very beautiful ship to play with.

The second leg
Hobart in Tasmania to Bluff in New Zealand - 1021 miles

25th. February, 2002 - Monday, 1630

Depart Hobart at last – we've been hanging around for a couple of days while some mysterious engineering problem got fixed.

Glad to be away. The ship has been untidy and dirty while we've been alongside and it was odd how badly I reacted to all the people coming aboard 'our' ship.

Some of the strangers were people delivering technical equipment or working on the ship but a lot of the strangers came to stay.

Quite a lot of good people, like Bones, Stuart, Malcolm Hay and Will Studd, got off at Hobart and the ship seems to be full of newbies now.

We old hands, with all of two weeks more seniority, mock them gently but persistently:

'You're only going to Rio de Janeiro?' (about 7,000 miles) 'Just a day-tripper, then?'

It is a relief to be free of land and on our way.

It is a relief to be free at last of that airport lounge transit feeling.

I've been killing time pleasantly in Hobart, but it's still dead time in the bars and the chandleries, buying heavy waterproofs, thermal underwear and new seaboots.

Money spent - quantities.

Alcohol drunk - lots.

Sleep hours missed – a great number.

Hated the shore-side untidiness, the lack of a routine, glad
to be at sea and at work again.

I want to get on with it.

Ruth and Martin Morant read this book in manuscript which improved
it a great deal. I am extremely grateful to them.

They pointed out, with amusement, that I completely omitted the most
spectacular thing that went on in Hobart, i.e. our training with
immersion suits and in survival techniques.

This exercise consisted of virtually the entire crew assembling on deck
in swimming costumes, old clothes and unlovely tee shirts and jumping
one by one into the cold waters of the harbour. The technique then was
to form larger and larger huddles, clustering together in the water to
conserve body heat. When we had experimented with this technique
and proved to our own satisfaction that it worked, we scrambled up
into rubber dinghies (not without difficulty) to see how claustrophobic
and fragile they are when viewed from the inside.

Obviously this training was necessary and advisable. It was also
interesting. I hadn't realised that thick ordinary clothes (even when
waterlogged) are so much much more effective in retaining heat than
thin ones. But I felt a bit cynical about the exercise because the
Southern Ocean is notorious for the most vicious seas on the globe and
our chances of successfully finding each other and huddling together in
the seas that we expected would be minimal.

Perhaps that is why I put nothing in my diary about it.

I wonder what else I left out?

*****

26/2 Tuesday

Dog watch 1800-2000. Spread main and forecourses and topsails – finally sailing – a cheer went up - motion much better, most over seasickness

27/2 Wednesday

I must write something about the current ship's company, perhaps starting by quoting Richard Henry Dana who described his various shipmates as mavericks, misfits, adventurers, alcoholics and illiterates.

Dana sailed round Cape Horn in the 1830s. His book about the experience is called "Two Years Before the Mast." He was an educated young man, a law student, but his eye sight failed him - he couldn't study any more - so he decided to run away to sea.

We have no apparent illiterates on board but the rest of Dana's categories seem spot-on.

They are a very experienced, fit and tough bunch - many of them with many days on Endeavour before they joined this time.

One played a significant role on a yacht that won its class in the celebrated Sydney-Hobart race.

Another was in the Royal Australian Navy and is an amateur naval historian. The average age of the crew and the level of experience both seem to have risen.

On the other hand, two very beautiful young women (Jane and Tiffany) came on board in Hobart and neither has sailed before. Nor has Bernard, a waiter from Sydney, who still speaks and perhaps thinks, like a Frenchman.

He has been in Australia for more than 20 years and gets very annoyed when his restaurant customers ask him when he is going home.

Australia <u>is</u> home for him and he speaks extremely accurate English, though still with a pronounced accent.

He has joined the foremast watch so that we have even more to amuse us than before.

It is pleasant enough on deck in the night and (by comparison with what happened after we left Fremantle) the weather is balmy. I have not been seriously cold or wet since we left Hobart. This afternoon was fabulous, bright, windy, with whitecaps on the water and the sun shining as if it were high summer. Albatrosses are no longer curiosities but they are still stunning to watch. They fly into the troughs of waves deliberately, almost dipping their wings in the water. But we never see them feed.

I did not know we were going to call at Bluff until about a day before we left Hobart. I was a bit surprised and irritated. I really do want to get on with it, to get to sail round Cape Horn - another shore-side interlude I can do without.

However, there are engine spares and an engineer and two film-makers to be collected at Bluff so we will have to stop there for a day or two. I need to buy more warm socks and notebooks and toothpaste and maybe send postcards to Rita and Josh.

28/2 - Thursday – morning watch.

A sky painted by a lunatic. Bright and dark-tipped clouds scudding across it. Fierce moon light glinting on an impatient ocean. A smoke of cloud across the moon's glaring, grinning face.

There was a lunar rainbow last night at 2100.

Good sailing – main course, fore course, fore topsail, jib, mizzen staysail – very well balanced at the wheel, just rounding up to windward – I had a great hour's helming in the moonlight – steering by the wind at 120 degrees, by and large. It was a south westerly wind but not cold. It rained when I got back on deck after a tea break. Then superb conditions in the morning, the sea shining as brightly as if it had just been invented, the blue sky washed clean by the night, the albatross re-discovering it can soar.

28th. February was my mother's birthday. I thought about her a lot that particular day and during the whole voyage. She would have appreciated the beauty of the best days - and she would have sympathised with me about the emptiness of the life, the lack of intellectual stimulus.

Out on the bowsprit again later, on bow-watch – in bright sunshine; wind blowing, sea blue with excitement and the albatrosses soaring round – not a bad way to spend the last bit of a long day.

1/3 - Friday

Yesterday I made no observation of latitude because of galley duty and wearing ship shortly before lunch – I could not find the time.

Unspeakably foul, last night's weather. Pouring with rain, up to 40 knots of wind – snugged down in the evening (finishing in the dark) to main course, fore course and main staysail.

Endeavour bucketed along – and my new boots and waterproofs made me reasonably comfortable.

But this morning was glorious. I needed dark glasses just to get up through the hatch.

3/3 - Sunday

The days, as always, running one into the other. Where has Saturday gone?

Chatted with Alex yesterday when he was relieving me on bow watch, c. 0600.

"I used to work in Perth's Central Park – great view, the ocean and the sky all blue, all blue - and I wanted to be out there – not stuck inside the office with the water cooler."

Alex (and Kate, Clare, Craig, Camilla and Fleur, are all starting a correspondence course on maritime matters (Australian Master 5) which takes them up to and beyond the Yachtmaster theory qualification from the UK.

Alex (and Craig) are wondering whether to crew or to cruise after all this is over. I think they will probably want to go on sailing or working with sailing ships professionally.

"It will give you another string to your bow," I said later to Craig when we talked about it.

Craig is obviously highly intelligent but he was seduced away from college into the internet game after a mere eight months of tertiary education.

He ended up helping to run Microsoft in Australia.

I think the puzzle of what to do with his life remains just that, a puzzle. It cannot be obvious. He has rather too many talents.

Overnight a series of fronts came through, making for bigger seas than the weather implies.

Now bright, very blowy, we've got two courses up and the main staysail.

Captain's rounds, yesterday – we all fear this, because Chris Blake is very very thorough and he is now very much in charge. Gary is still on board but he and Captain Dai are going to leave us, which is a shame.

Chris insists on cleanliness and is quite ruthless if he does not find it. Captain Cook was much the same. My watchmates and I work pretty hard to keep the areas allocated to us clean. Especially on Saturdays.

What I want to know is, did the Captain really plant that chewing gum which he found under a table, where I know I had cleaned the previous morning? I would not put it past him.

He certainly homed in on it remarkably efficiently and I cannot, in my right mind, imagine that any member of the Endeavour's crew would park chewing gum under the table when he/she knew the routine, knew the emphasis on cleanliness which is part of the Endeavour ethos.

Interesting. I will ask him one day.

I feel much more at ease with Chris than I did on the BBC trip. He greeted me rather warmly when I turned up again in Fremantle and he messes with us every day - we see a lot of him in an informal context, which has helped to break the ice.

The administrative load, of running the Endeavour Foundation as well as Endeavour, is a considerable burden and he is always on top of the navigational and sailing processes as well (I think he would say those were the easy bits).

Like everyone on board or associated with Endeavour, he works bloody hard.

On deck 1600 – greeted by a double rainbow. "Rainbows never fail to give me pleasure," I said, to no one in particular.

Good sailing in big swells from the SW. More than 80 minutes on the helm, which was very stiff indeed, we were struggling.

A waking dream:

Paris now – an aperitif? No, it is too early – they are washing the streets – it is dawn (do they still do that?) I am there with A., who is the same age as when I met her. She has not changed at all. I am twenty years older but it doesn't matter. Am I leaving her after a night of illicit passion? Are we coming back to a hotel after a night of celebration, to start the new morning in each other's arms. I still miss her. How ridiculous. In October it will be seventeen years since she left me.

And I never ever went with her to Paris.

3/3 - Sunday - middle watch

The heave and swell of the moon-washed, moon-spilled sea in the shiny darkness.

The bruising sea.

The swathed anonymous figures of all my watchmates wrapped up in oilskins. They are almost indistinguishable. David (very tall) and Clare (very small) are the only two who stand out. I mistook Glen for Sarah, which was not appreciated.

The ship is still full of my memories of people who were on board with me for my first trip, last year (2001). Moonbeam, from the BBC trip, is still on board for me. So are Sharon and Jenny (and Sam, oddly enough. I didn't know Sam well.)

A privilege to be out here, last night. We are already further south than most people in the world will ever go (45 degrees of southern latitude).

The moonlight highlighting the rigging and its beauty.

The pelting, ice-cold rain sneaking in under the cloud banks with squalls of up to 40 knots and the wind howling as the ship almost rolls its gunwales under and the decks grow slick and dangerous with spray.

30-40 knots of wind most days – sail plan virtually unchanged – worst rolling ever. Impossible to move without danger – breakages and spillages during supper. Waves more than six metres high.

Worse by middle watch – the wildest night yet.

The weather built up through the watch, touching 60 knots by 0315 – then we wore ship in some confusion and stonking great seas.

Two watches on deck and all the idlers and Andy got mislaid somewhere, at the end – Tig rushed about looking for him, in alarm – it was the sort of night you could lose someone overboard and not notice.

The mizzen staysail backed when the preventer jammed as we tried to turn so the boat wouldn't turn and the wind couldn't fill the forecourse which was also not sheeted – I would have been worried if I'd been in command.

A fore and aft rigged small boat would have been in trouble.

However, Endeavour was as solid as a rock, completely unphased by it all. I get the feeling she is a ship that will look after us.

Chris Blake, who has seen it all before, very cool in command (and splendidly audible – if he shouts, you hear it. Thank goodness for that.)

I asked Sarah about all this a day or too later and she confirmed that it is not a threat when you back a sail or a couple of sails like that or take your time completing the wearing manoeuvre and getting the ship around on to its new course. She shrugged it off.

"Normal," she said. "Just routine."

So – I am learning what a big heavy old sailing vessel can handle. However, it would be a mistake to be too blasé about it. These seas and conditions can bite and complacency is always one of the sailor's worst enemies.

Impossible to sleep afterwards – too much adrenalin – we were all very psyched up by the conditions and our struggles with them - we talked about it a bit and then Alex settled down to write up his diary to put himself to sleep.

Oscar Wilde claimed that a diary should provide something sensational to read on the train.

Alex's is evidently not that sort of diary.

Two hours good sleep, then breakfast now (1030 ship's time) passing Solander Island – a great bleak spiky lump of rock with shark like spikes around it – the seas still very substantial.

Solander was the distinguished biologist who sailed on Endeavour with Captain Cook. He was a Fellow of the Royal Society and he survived the voyage and got back to England in reasonable health, together with all his notebooks and specimens.

Cook's first great voyage on the Endeavour, with its botanists and biologists, its astronomer and the young and precocious presence of the wealthy young Joseph Banks and his two greyhounds, could be described as the first British voyage of exploration with a real scientific purpose.

Cook and his companions brought home genuine scientific samples, suggestions and results. The journey was not just an imperialist foray into unknown oceans, to explore them and to conquer fresh territories.

In the morning, cleaning stations on the eighteenth century deck which was all awash last night when a wave came unexpectedly down the one hatch which is still kept open – I heard the fuss from my hammock as I tried to go to sleep.

I thought about getting up to help to clear the mess and then I just ignored it all and rolled over and went to sleep.

You can do that if you are desperate from tiredness. And we had to stand middle watch yet again.

4/3 - Monday 1100

Engines started to get in to Bluff by 1715

Lots of happy gossip in the mess – an attack of the Channels, which is when people get slightly light-headed at the thought of seeing land again.

Out into Bluff in the evening and sampled two pubs with Tony, Steve, Joe the mud doctor and Peter the proper doctor – I had no New Zealand dollars so I owe Tony two drinks and Peter one.

The first pub was so rough it made the second look smart and sophisticated.

This was quite an achievment, given that the second pub was large, bleak, nasty, crowded with badly mis-conceived decorations, littered with juke boxes and gambling machines, full of cigarette smoke and populated mainly by the local alcoholics.

Steve is about 29 years old, has a gentle, rather round face. He wears a purple scarf across his mouth when it's cold or sometimes as a headband – an odd touch.

He is sturdily built, un-fey – he might be a trucker or yet another internet/software engineer – the ship is full of youngish people like that.

Steve is, I think, on mainmast watch so our paths have hardly crossed at all. He sleeps when I am on duty and vice versa. We are awake simultaneously only at meals which, for the most part, we eat with our respective watchmates.

On Endeavour you live with and within your watch. The rest of the ship's company remain relative strangers.

Anyway, he wouldn't say how he lived or where he comes from, even though we were having an amicable encounter (our first) in the pub at Bluff on the first evening.

"All that's over. I've cut myself off from that."

He thinks he will get off in South America. There may be work for him in the oil industry.

He said that he was on Endeavour aiming to cut himself off, to find motivation, to find a purpose.

"Have you none?"

"I think I'm put here on Earth just to do certain things ......"

I never found out what they were. Did someone interrupt us? Was I too tired to remember them? Was he too tired to tell me about them?

I shall never know.

Odd, and rather poignant, to remember such an unfulfilled conversation, such a promising beginning to a debate.

Tig has a gentle and kind face, when he's not stomping fish.

He and Kate giggle together as if they were the same age. He is actually about eight years older but they have become a number and make no secret of it.

Tig has a strangely monotonous and muffled way of speaking but a serious glint in his eye.

I suspect he gets himself into fights and could have been a real tearaway if he had not been at sea. His brother was, I believe, a handful. He also came on Endeavour for some while and settled down when he finished his stint with her.

I think Tig and Kate have probably run out of money for hotels and spend quite a lot of time cuddling or communing together on the boat, in public view. This is not strictly in conformity with the boat's non-touch policy but who cares – Glen and Anastasia are much the same.

What I loved was Kate's reply when I was trying to organize a rota in the watchleader's absence the other day. I had the work-sheet in front of me and was preparing to write down her details so that she would get a wake-up call at some ungodly hour in the morning..

"What's your hammock number now?" I asked.

She giggled, not nervously but with a 19 year old's chilling determination.

"I shall be in Tig's cabin," she said.

"Which bunk?" I asked with a not entirely straight face, because he shares that cabin with both Andy Law and John Highmore.

"The middle one," she said.

"I don't think I'll write that down," I said.

Of course, there was a mix up with our night watch on Wednesday – only three people from foremast watch were on board, not enough to organize the necessary duties alongside. I am a little annoyed about having to do extra duty - because it could easily have been organized if we had thought ahead. The moment we reach harbour, the bonds of loyalty and duty break down - and they need not. The people who are in hotels on shore know that they are ignoring their responsibilities. They would never do that at sea. It is an interesting (and distressing) phenomenon.

Tony, in the pub – talking, like Steve, about purpose, energy, dedication – what the trip meant to him, how beautiful and addictive it is. He is the last person in the world to embroider or even to express his feelings openly. 'A grumpy old git from Yorkshire' is how he describes himself.

He has a sensational black beard. He looks like a boyar from the Eisenstein film about Ivan the Terrible.

Rossi, the one American on board, is from Boston and has rashly invited me to come and stay. What a temptation! I loved Boston when I was there working with MIT in the early 1980s. One of the few American cities where I would be happy to live.

Bluff, New Zealand

Work on the quayside, as we prepared to set off across the Pacific

There is always a bad day in a long voyage. The day you want to give up. The day you want to forget.

For me, it was the last day in Bluff, in New Zealand, the day before we sailed again, to tackle the Pacific. This is what I wrote and it contradicts almost everything I said in the emails I sent the same day.

Mine was a very private sort of despair, full of frustration and anger. I wanted very much to keep it to myself, until now:

8/3 - Friday

We leave for Cape Horn tomorrow. I have a nasty feeling that the Prime Minister of New Zealand is going to come down to see us off. This is my last chance to back out of this idiotic enterprise and I am sitting in a strange, empty, echoing café on the southern extremity of the southern island listening to schmaltzy versions of pop classics like Beethoven's Ninth and thinking seriously about it all and wondering whether backing out is really an option. I have my second glass of red wine in front of me and will very soon have a third.

As I look out through the rain on the windows, I see a landscape and a grey, grey sea that take me right back to Cornwall, where I used to spend holidays with my family, to unhappily thoughtful sessions, by myself, in pubs overlooking the sea, when I was younger and still married and it was so hard to know who I was and what I was doing and why. This café is called 'Land's End'.

I was always good at 'angst'. Behind the bonhomie and the bravado and the competence, there has always been anxiety, indecision, perhaps inadequacy. I am just very good at bluffing myself and other people.

Also, at facing up to a challenge.

Above the rocky, barren sea-shore in front of me, a yellow lettered signpost announces how far it is to the Equator and New York and Sydney and London and Hobart and Stewart Island.

It doesn't say how far it is to Cape Horn, but I know that already. It is too far by half, all the way across the Pacific. Fifty or sixty days of being back on that ship without touching land.

It is going to be a lifetime.

I think I would rather be almost anywhere than here, just at this moment.

I was on gangway watch last night, first till 2300 and then from 0600 and sleep deprivation makes me (and everyone else) negative, scratchy and frustrated. Even the little problems become big and the large problems become huge and overwhelming.

Also, we are so bad at coping when we are not sailing, when the ship is attached uncomfortably, unnaturally, to the shore.

It tends to be a bit of a shambles and yesterday was no exception.

The day before yesterday, we laboriously struck the t'gallant masts, to lower the centre of gravity of the ship and to reduce the sail plan to something more suitable for the Southern Ocean, where courses and topsails will provide quite enough speed in the big winds that we expect. Captain Cook would have done the same.

This operation involved virtually the whole ship's company and a lot of very dangerous and skilled work aloft by members of the professional crew. It took most of the day.

Today, after a morning's energetic cleaning and a hurried lunch, three or four hundred schoolchildren arrived, apparently without warning, and had to be shown around a ship that was half-dismantled for re-furbishing, re-packing, re-invigoration. I was busy, energetically sanding down and then re-varnishing seven large spars (the two t'gallant masts and several other spare spars and yards). I thought not only that I was doing a good job but that it was more important to get that done than anything else I could possible have been doing and deeply resented two unexpected and unexplained and sudden decisions, that I should be on galley duty after lunch (with the varnish hardening on the brush) and that I should show lots of the children round later in the afternoon.

Unfortunately, I made my dislike for these decisions and my impatience very obvious indeed to our current watch-leader, with whom I do not get on. As I have often regretted, I have no gift for keeping my mouth shut.

Eventually, I got back to my masts and (almost) finished everything I wanted to do.

Pete the Fish, meanwhile, slaved away at cleaning the side of the ship, perching himself on makeshift stages tied to the deck rails, and then fell into the harbour rather quietly, without a shout or much of a splash.

There was no safety line rigged, there was no rope ladder near to him, he was not wearing a life jacket and he had no safety man. There were no lifebelts around.

Fortunately, Andy and Tony and I were within earshot. It was only chance that we were close and that Andy and Tony are two of the strongest people on the entire crew, so we had the power to get him out quickly in spite of the lack of life-saving equipment.

Andy grabbed Pete by the wrist.

I grabbed a length of rope as I ran towards him and tied a big bowline in it and dropped it to him. Once he got his foot into the loop, he could help to push himself upwards.

With Tony's help, we hoisted him the eight or ten feet up from the water to the quay.

"My boots are filling up," was all he said whilst in the water.

He was wearing brand new Dubarry boots and he had been very proud of them.

Out of the water, he was still in shock.

He took his boots off and Tony brought him a cup of tea with sugar and he took a gulp of it and ignored the blanket which Tony had brought him and schlepped off, limping, to shower and change his clothes.

He went back to work on the side of the ship afterwards, which was over and beyond the call of duty.

But what interested me was that our watch-leader didn't move. She was sitting nearby, on the quay, while all this happened, just a few yards away. She didn't take the trouble to come to see if Pete (a member of her watch) was OK, she didn't express any regrets to him or show concern about his welfare. She just went on chatting. I don't think she even stood up to see what was happening.

Jon Preston, later, used the words 'factional', 'divisive', and 'favouritism' when talking about her. It is a bit worrying that Alex, whom I like so much, and Craig and Clare, seem so much in her pocket.

Pete raised the whole question about our watchleader last night while we were on gangway watch together. I shut him up.

"It's not worth talking about, or thinking about," I said firmly. "It's very silly."

I don't like to gossip and I didn't want to talk about it. But of course it's not 'very silly' at all. It's rather important.

If she destroys the unity of the watch and especially if I get too isolated in my watch, I shall have a very unhappy and lonely time over the next two or three months.

I am trying now to see where everyone stands but I am also very unwilling to spend my time trying to win an unwinnable battle – I don't do that. I would rather abandon the field and pretend I never wanted to fight than start a battle I can't ever win.

"She's lost it," said Jon at lunchtime.

Apparently she is trying to get two other members of the permanent crew to tidy up the cabin which the three of them share.

She has has called a formal meeting for that purpose!

I don't think treating her cabin-mates like naughty children is likely to be a great success.

That rant probably did me a lot of good – it certainly took a lot of time.

On Endeavour and my other long distance sailing trips, I normally kept notes only in small, battered notebooks which I could keep with me and use whenever opportunity offered.

My comments got terser and terser, as the pages got smaller and more crowded and the journey wore on.

Towards the end of any journey, almost everything that needed to be said seemed already to have been said. We all ended up, as Dana noticed, so over-familiar with each other that we were 'talked out', speechless, mute with frustration at our own contiguity.

That long diatribe about our watch-leader could never have fitted into my small notebook.

I had the use of Martin Morant's lap-top computer for much of the voyage round Cape Horn and, in Bluff on that day, I settled down in the cafe with it for an hour or two. I even asked permission from the proprietors and plugged it into mains electricity.

The cameraman and sound man working for Peter Weir (and shooting for National Geographic on the side) came into the cafe to have a last proper meal before they embarked with us for Cape Horn.

I only knew them by sight at that time, so we hardly spoke. I finished up my wine and packed up the computer and started to trudge back to the ship, all bile (or at least a lot of it) thoroughly spent.

The trouble was that I had no stomach for an extended campaign against someone on board – it would have made unhappiness for me, as well as for my watchmates and others. It would have spoiled the whole thing for everyone. It was just not on.

So how was I to get out of a relationship with my watch-leader that had turned confrontational?

Move watch ...... if necessary, that's what I was determined to do.

Much as I adored my watchmates. I thought it would be better to move to another watch than to stay with a watchleader with whom I clashed.

But I was going to stay on board Endeavour, of course. I think I always knew I had to go on round Cape Horn instead of quitting.

*****

Furling one of the topsails - Martin Morant is second from the left

The third leg

Bluff in New Zealand to Cape Horn (5,349 miles) and on via the Falkland Islands and Rio Grande to Rio de Janeiro - 6,323 miles .

8/3- Friday

Our last night in Bluff, our last night ashore for a long long time – farewell piss up with Gary in the pub, (he is not now coming round the Horn with us, which is a shame) and Claire the Penguin played pool all night with concentration, single-mindedness and much frowning (and always with a cigarette dangling from her lips) - she looked like a very young gangster's moll.

9/3 – Saturday

Hard to get back on the boat – harder each time; there are two more such moments (Rio and the Azores) – perhaps the Falklands as well, but I won't have any alternative there - it's virtually impossible to get away from the Falklands except by the way you came in. I don't think jumping ship in the Falklands is much of an option, however desperate I am to get off.

Gary was much nicer than he seemed at first. People liked him, especially (I think) the younger people. Perhaps that is one of the problems with all this – I am really too old to be bossed about?

I thought Gary a bit too full of himself to start with but I came to respect him a lot. He knows his stuff and he loves sailing, he loves the ship itself. A pity not to have him on board for Cape Horn. Reading between the lines, it seems probable that someone has fallen out with someone but who with whom and why it is not for me either to know or to speculate.

But I was sorry to see the back of him and so were the youngsters. He had been the Master of the Duyfken, another replica ship, of an even older type than Endeavour and I think he went back to her after his disappointing involvement with Endeavour.

Departure day pretty frantic – a great deal of work in a short time; loading the pinnace on board and the spars, recovering the re-furbished fore topsail and forecourse from the Town Hall (where they've been checked and thoroughly overhauled and mended and where extra reefing lines have been sewn in), hoisting in and lashing up the fizz boat, re-attaching the big fenders; we were off by about 1145, which was bloody amazing but the celebratory cannon outside the harbour misfired and went off with a pop instead of a bang. That was a shame. There were quite a lot of people waiting and they would have appreciated the noise and the gesture of farewell. We didn't have time to load and fire another.

As we waited, interminably, to depart Bluff, orders shouted, lines cast off in a very particular order, fenders recovered and stowed with some effort - at the last minute, quite unexpectedly, the rather non-descript gang of young men who were hanging around on the quay suddenly took off their shirts and sweaters and bare-chested in the cool damp day, gave us a rousing haka which brought tears to my eyes. It was a wonderful moment. I don't think anyone on board knew that it had been planned. I certainly didn't.

So we motored steadily away from the quay in Bluff with cheers and that emblematic, ancestral, sculptural farewell dance still echoing behind us. The good wishes emanating from New Zealand were so vigorous, so palpable, that I wondered frivolously if they would have filled the sails if we'd unfurled them.

And I wrote nothing at all about it in my diary, treasuring the memory 'in petto', hoarding it in my heart, not writing it down.

Interesting, that? I wonder why.

Of course, once you write things down, you do not have to remember them.

That haka, I very much wanted to remember, for a long, long time.

I slept through till we got to Stewart Island c. 1600, which looked lovely. We went into the bay under power and circled round rather cautiously. The Prime Minister was there (so there was some truth in the rumour about her seeing us off) and we fired off three more cannon, which did not misfire - I went up the foremast to bend on the course, help with the topsail as well.

Suppertime – v. tired – wrote up these notes on deck. Can I stand 60 days like this?

Middle watch tonight and for 8 more days (!). We are a bit unlucky there - it's the worst watch and we would normally only have to do it for a week.

Around 7.30 pm

Our last glimpse of New Zealand – what land, when land next?

Courtesy flag down just as I go to my hammock. We are now out of New Zealand's waters.

10/3 - Sunday

Gorgeous bright evening – huge swells, chill wind, bowling along – everything set except jibs and spritsails (they're working on the jibs)

Wanted to be outside scribbling these notes but it was very cold and Tony was there and wanted to talk about the rigging. It is so difficult to get any privacy. The watch was v. quiet (v. cold) on middle watch this morning. No badinage at all. Are we talking to each other as easily as we used to?

Alex and Craig baited Glen enjoyably at the morning meeting, so maybe it really was just the overnight cold and normal idiocy will soon be resumed. I hope so. We need it out here.

There was a good crowd of dolphins on view but only briefly – by the time I got on deck, most of them were gone and I just saw two of them, streaking away under the bows like ribbons of phosphorescence or huge fast tadpoles.

After the meeting, we all cleaned like mad and I spent two and a half hours in the galley, missing most of my watch. So I have not been much on deck today, which is a pity.

11/3 - Monday - 0411

Moonless again, but not cold.

A sailor's breeze. Good (moderate) speed. Light winds, no rain, rising barometer.

A canopy of canvas against a dark sky, every sail swelling heaving, panting and the rigging skeletal and strong as cobwebs pulling the ship up towards its centre.

Much hilarity on deck tonight - everyone was warm enough. We've all got new heavy waterproofs which fit us properly. However, it is still a bore getting them on and off.

"I love the sound of velcro in the morning," said Bernard, splendidly parodying the line about napalm in 'Apocalypse Now.'

And it is true - the loud tearing noises as we undo the Velcro to get our gear on and off are characteristic of the way we live on this ship.

The eighteenth century mess deck resounds to loud ripping sounds as a whole watch removes its heavy waterproofs and rushes for breakfast down below in the twentieth century mess.

12/3 - Tuesday - 0730

Overcast, light winds, pretty cold – very dull middle watch but Alex suddenly amazingly chatty and lively, as he was in yesterday's forenoon watch when he whooped and gestured like a monkey as he distributed bananas to everyone. Craig answered him whoop for whoop and the two of them got on the helm together, threatening to wear ship to get the wind in the right direction for Craig's haircut.

Sarah, who was officer of the watch, was slightly non-plussed by all this silliness, blinking in the sunlight with mild incomprehension. She takes her work seriously (as she should).

This morning, Alex was still chatty (Craig less so – there is a 'flu going round and Nigel has been poorly). His language and his ways of speaking interest me.

"Bananas, eh? Wicked? My favourite shenanigans food?"

Everything ends up as a question in modern-speak. The upwards intonation at the end of a sentence? Is it from televison? (I heard Nigel describe making his own diesel fuel the other day, a little mini technical lecture - I didn't know you could. But it all came out as a series of questions.)

Shenanigans is both a favourite Alex word and an activity.

Shenanigans can be sexual or just playful. Alex, like Craig, is in flight from the sort of life lacking in shenanigans.

His vocabulary is enterprising. I hadn't heard the word 'shenanigans' for years before I came on board this boat.

'Grunts' (what I call ordinary voyage crew) are 'squeezers' to him. I must ask him why.

I did, eventually – it goes back to the talented Mr. Ripley, our watch leader for a few days between Fremantle and Hobart. "He had a great jaw line," said Kate eagerly when his name came up. And Ripley was indeed very good looking, tall, slender, with curly hair and crinkly laugh lines round his eyes. He is also the only full time square rigger sail maker in Australia and I rather liked him. I was sorry he wasn't sailing further with us

Apparently Ripley asked Alex one night watch to go down to the twentieth century mess area to get back some of the watch who were spending too much time on their tea break.

"He said squeezers," said Alex. "I just picked it up. He said 'go get those squeezers'."

What does it mean?

"I think he meant plonkers, wankers, you know, too much time squeezing the Big Man?"

Right, thanks Alex .... too much information?

> Alex's turn of phrase can be sharp or sometimes wistful. He mislaid a glove, as I did, then he found it again.

> "It was like a kitten that had gone missing coming home," he said. "I was so pleased to see it. It was like finding an animal again, a lost animal."

> Alex is having trouble growing his beard. The moustache is so fair it is invisible. The rest is indeterminate. After more than a month, it looks just as if he hasn't bothered to shave for a day or two.

> In one of his woolly hats and his granny specs., he looks very Russian, straight out of Chekhov. His surname is Russian, or eastern European.

> Does the almost incessant joking shield him from other questions and emotions? It is certainly relentless and exaggerated (and can be tiresome).

> In some ways, I am glad to see him back in form, bumptious, loud, silly – very much himself. Unfortunately he is now so mixed up with our watchleader (they shared a

bedroom in Bluff) that I am not speaking as openly to him as I once might have. Pity.

There is always a stage, in every journey, when I despair of it ending and repine (?is that the right word?) to be somewhere else.

I get irritated very readily, esp. with routine (and the ship's flu is around).

In other words, I am not enjoying myself much at the moment.

Talked, in the middle of the night, to Kate about school and what she studied there. She is going on to study sports medicine or something close to it, which should suit her. She does pushups with enthusiasm and can climb and kiss the block (the Endeavour fitness test) without any difficulty, though she uses her legs as well as her arms, unlike the men.

We talked about poetry, which she says she does not like.

Yet she sings along with her CDs and tapes all the time. She knows all the words of all those verses. I pointed out that verse can be poetry and vice versa. Poetry is in pop songs as well as text books and anthologies.

She was not convinced but she may well have stored the comment away for future reference. I think she is like that.

I suppose I cited Bob Dylan and the Beatles as examples? They are the usual suspects.

Would she willingly listen to either? That's my generation's music. She will, at the least, have heard of them.

I was a bit taken aback by what she told me about one of her set texts for High School English which was, believe it or not, the film "Shakespeare in Love."

(A 'set text'?)

She said she did not like analysing it.

I am not at all surprised – there is nothing in it to analyse;
it is an amusing romp, that is all, not something to study –
there are no hidden depths to discover.

There was always a shortage of mugs on board Endeavour. You go to make a cup of tea or coffee and find that all the mugs have migrated to the shipwright's work space, the boatswain's cabin or somewhere equivalent. The professional crew are notorious for hiding quantities of cups away.

At the morning meetings, Glen is always threatening to throw all the mugs overboard if they can't be kept clean and sorted and they aren't stored where they belong.

So, in Invercargill, I tried to buy myself a mug - and failed. Nothing suitable seemed to be about.

In Bluff, in desperation, as my last day on shore came to an end, I went into the little stationery shop which is also a newsagent.

The lady behind the counter asked what I was looking for and I told her. She didn't sell mugs of course, but she gave me one of her own glass mugs and I still treasure it and use it most days when I am in London. It survived all the way across the Pacific and came back to Whitby, in Yorkshire, with me.

She wouldn't take any money and I promised her a postcard from Rio de Janeiro to say thank you.

When I sat down in a street cafe in Rio to write it, other members of the Endeavour crew kept walking past and I kept stopping them and telling them the story about my mug.

In the end, I think her card was signed by six or seven Cape Horners as well as me.

It was actually quite the wrong sort of mug for a long journey on a sailing ship. It had a very narrow base and toppled over with the slightest roll. My watchmates hid it from me for quite a while because it was such a nuisance! But I still like it - it has good associations.

It is hanging on the wall opposite as I type this out.

13/3 – Wednesday - the Ides of March

Still on middle watch.

Starboard engine now unuseable – it gave up just 4 days out, with a bent pushrod (or something), which is pretty terminal (at least until the Falklands)

Steering odd under power – unbalanced with only one engine running.

Not enough sleep – sail-handling till after 2000 last night. On duty again at 0400.

Today is grey, overcast, calm – we are motoring. There is no chance of astro sights.

The ship is full of scribblers – does everyone on board intend to publish a diary? Or are they writing yet more contributions for the Endeavour web-site?

Bernard has been reading my copy of the Rime of the Ancient Mariner out loud with his strong French accent – the result is *epatant*, stunning!

This morning he read a bit of it out loud on the ship's tannoy, to wake us all up!

It is a colourful experience, just to listen to him. He is a colourful character.

Graeme, in Main Mast watch, is also a heck of a character – he speaks in an incomprehensible (and very quiet) Scottish accent and has long, lank hair and limbs – red woolly cap., brown woolly beard, brown tinted glasses, brown knees.

In six weeks, no one has seen Graeme wash – he always wears soiled once-white cotton shorts and the rest of his wardrobe seems to come from lost property. He wears no shoes and his bare dirty feet are horrific to contemplate yet he is the most generous of men with his time, help, assistance (and advice).

His skills are as a climber/rigger – I believe he works full time as a railwayman and is about 41 years old.

He certainly knows Endeavour better than almost anyone, including most members of the professional crew.

This is, I think, the third or fourth time he has been on board.

14/3 - Middle watch

It rained – afternoon ditto. Waterproof gloves proved not to be.

Looked out at the sea (force 5), loads of albatrosses, thought of the haka as we departed Bluff – I wept.

No one will ever take that beauty away from me.

That moment of surprise and beauty - all that energy, in our honour.

It is exactly what I came for.

Alex suddenly silent. For a whole day. His lips sealed. Why? I did ask him but he has, apparently, vowed to keep siilent for 24 hours so he couldn't tell me.

I suppose someone suggested he talks too much!

Did I have a cold or a small flu in and after Bluff?

Today, it was as if a cloud had lifted.

I can laugh again.

We had two Thursday 14ths., because of the dateline.

The first culminated (climaxed?) in a mass moon on the main course yard. Alex, no longer vowing silence, and Dougal the boatswain were among the ring leaders – foremast boasted about four arses out of the eight.

Interesting how anonymous bottoms are ... only Hans (who inadvisedly looked around as all the photographs were taken) will be at all recognizable.

Language again, how the young Australians talk.

"Coz.," "bro.," – used as greetings.

Snaggers, (sausages), hard yakka, the mutt's nuts, jocks and socks, chubbies, stiffies, soggy and foggy – I like the vitality of Australian and New Zealand expressions and language. It is invigorating.

Still 14/3

Dull middle watch (no time on helm). Southern Cross now looking like Crux at last. Scorpio rather wonderful, in the ascendant (Orion not glimpsed).

No albatross today – yesterday there were a dozen or more. Where do they go, why do they follow us anyway?

A mystery.

Gorgeous at lunchtime. Force 6?

The horizon blinding under the noon sun. Mountains of white tops alongside us. Bright, bright sunshine – the sea azure, active, agitated.

Growler waters? That is what we are told. We are asked to keep an extra careful look out (but growlers don't show on the radar and certainly would not be spotted in the dark. If we hit one, it's just too bad ....)

Growlers are little icebergs, the little bits which fall off the very big icebergs and lurk virtually below the surface, waiting for you to run into them.

If you hit them hard, they can do big damage.

Not really cold, perhaps 8-9 degrees C. The wind is from the south and chill, but it is no as bad as off West Australia.

Few dolphins, almost no whales. No tuna caught. Today no birds.

Hello? Anyone about?

This is a very lonely ocean.

Young Ally (Alastair?), another character, the current boatswain's mate, about 19 years old, with ultra-dirty overalls and filthy, tarry hands leaving fingerprints all over the nice clean lavatories, which Bernard and I attended to so carefully this morning.

Ally has a deep voice, of which he is proud and a long, thick book of folk-songs which he sings with great enthusiasm and volume, whenever asked.

But there is still a lot of the little boy in him — how possibly to describe that gesture and the noise he made as he leaned his grizzled head on a young woman's shoulder and howled an apology like a wolf or a coyote - (but what had he done? Why did it happen? I don't know, I don't remember - I don't think I ever knew, I just observed the gesture with some amusement. He has a lot of charm as well as youth and fiery red curly hair.)

Trying to work out when we will reach Cape Horn - there is a competition for the most accurate estimate. I worked out our daily averages so far:

Fremantle to Hobart, 5/2 to 19/2 = 14 days = 2114 nautical miles =151 nautical miles per day

Hobart to Bluff, 26/2 to 4/3 = 6 days = 1021 nautical miles = 170 nautical miles per day

Big winds on both of those sections of the voyage. How much can we rely on big winds from the right direction on the way across the rest of the Pacific?

Bluff to our current position, 10/3 to 17/3 = 9 days = 139 nautical miles per day

Those averages do not tell me much. There is a fifty percent margin of error.

But, if I back-calculate on the distance from the Horn and allow for adverse winds late in the passage, I think we might pass Cape Horn on or around 24 April – late in the day.

Everyone in the mess was vastly amused by my estimate, which was the most pessimistic by far. Some people seemed to think we'd be at Cape Horn in a couple of weeks.

In fact, we reached Cape Horn on 16 April, early in the day and Pete the Fish predicted our arrival most accurately. Bluff to the Horn took 39 days and I had estimated 47.

I think my estimate might have been very close if Endeavour had not used its surviving engine so much in the early stages of the Pacific crossing. But then I would say that, wouldn't I?

15/3 - Friday 1236

No chance of a noon sight with my sextant – overcast, grey, the sea alive w. white-tops, no albatrosses, real sailor's wind (last watch averaged 9 knots for their 4 hours) and a lot of sail up the masts ie foremast staysail, topsail and course, main staysail, topmast staysail, topsail, course and mizzen staysail.

In the night we had the mizzen topsail and the spritsail set which was too much. It gusted to 38 knots apparent, about 45 knots true.

15/3 – Friday (continued)

Grey sea, grey sky, a few small grey birds in the distance and the most violent topaz blue in the wake and where the waves break beside us.

Penguins glimpsed? A small flurry of snow? A half dozen small (spinner) dolphins playing at our bow.

Later: not spinners apparently – duskies. John Anderson, the sound recordist for the PeterWeir/National Geographic film team, knows all about dolphins.

24hr. speed record at 1600 – average 7.76 knots for a whole day between yesterday and today. But on Saturday, the Captain announced another new record – 7.9 knots over a 24 hr. period.

"190 miles," he said triumphantly, "it's not enough! I want 200."

See later on – he got it - and a bit more.

My watchmates and I have been cleaning the male heads, the lavatories, all this week. Very boring, but they are now very clean.

When they are finished, before they are inspected, I can prevent anyone (even my other watchmates) entering, for fear they are defiled.

This small exercise of power, this small span of privacy, is very welcome. This morning, I brought my coffee in and drank it, luxuriating in the space and solitude.

16/3 - Saturday - 1502

No sights possible today. Very grey and misty – the swells smaller, the wind about 20-25 knots, very manageable conditions. Dull!

I like it better when it's hairy ....

Captain's Rounds – and we got a good outcome. The heads and the galley were clean enough for him. National Geographic were filming their documentary in his wake and John and Paul, the cameraman, said that the seriousness with which Bernard and I responded to the Captain's comments was fairly comical.

I have this slightly disconcerting vision of myself on prime time television dressed in rags, probably slightly unshaven, energetically scrubbing down a ship's lavatories while holding on to avoid falling over (it is still pretty rough).

Not quite the image of myself I most treasure?

Captain Noodle (old nickname for Glen) – perfect.

Jane Inglis has pictures of him when he had long hair.

Bernard did not appreciate that 'noodle' means simpleton and not just a form of Chinese food.

17/3 - St. Patrick's Day

Sunday – layday - stars bright in our (last) middle watch.

I celebrated my 59th. birthday at 54 degrees 40 minutes south, 163 degrees 28 minutes west.

I breakfasted on cinnamon rolls and bacon and scrambled eggs and was favoured with a rousing chorus of Happy Birthday and three loud cheers in the mess – John Highmore was the cheerleader, perhaps inevitably.

Jane organized a birthday card for me and a present of a few sweets. Much appreciated. I enjoy Jane's company much more now that I know she is no longer to be our watch-leader.

A beautiful sunny day and I caught local noon by the skin of my teeth and lots of good luck . Very little wind. Conditions are so changeable down here.

Endeavour is flying an Irish courtesy flag today, which is a nice touch.

Kate asked me how old I was and which birthday I was celebrating. So I told her.

"59? That's nearly sixty. My Granny's in her Sixties."

Thanks, Kate – she also says I sound like the Speaking Clock - I wonder what she means by that? That I speak pedantically and precisely, elocute clearly? Anyway, I am sure it was not intended as a compliment ......

She is admirably blunt sometimes.

Kate: You snore, Jay.

J. Yes, I know

(Pause)

J. Actually, I don't know, really. I've never heard myself.

(Pause)

Kate: You're lucky.

(Laughter)

J. I brought some spare ear plugs - for anyone sleeping near to me.

Nigel: Try sticking them up your nose.

(Laughter)

Not a word since about my snoring, but Craig (my nearest hammock-neighbour) now sleeps with his head towards my feet.

18/3 - Monday

Craig's birthday − he is also the new watch leader and was greeted with a chorus of Happy Birthday when he called on us to muster and number off at four in the morning in the middle of a pitch black howling ocean.

That banal ditty has never sounded better.

Jane is not now with us − a relief. We are to rotate the watch-leader's duties.

"It's more relaxed already," said Alex a few minutes after 0400, as Craig made his first dispositions.

Then, catching my warning look, "I'd better button my shit-stirring mouth."

We have gone through four watch leaders in 6 weeks. but we are the hot watch, according to Nat and Geo, the two film-makers, who are obviously fascinated by the social dynamics (and mechanics) of life on board.

19/3 - Tuesday

Damp, foggy, quiet. Did nothing happen?

Stoicism and humour – two qualities attributed to me by Claire, the young doctor on the BBC trip, in an e-mail earlier this year.

They both seem to have deserted me today.

20/3 - Wednesday

4675 miles so far and we are still only one third of the way across the Pacific.

Dawn was beautiful, almost worth all the monotony and frustration of this featureless life.

It has been grey and overcast or foggy and windless. We haven't glimpsed the new moon which is already overdue. But this morning I was out on the bowsprit, alone over the ocean, and the coming of the sun split the grey sky wide across the rolling dripping bow, streaks of pink grey and grey pink, even a band of blue up high and the glimmer of reflected sunlight on the base of the cumulo nimbus mountains of cloud up towards the stratosphere. It was fabulous and I stayed up there for twice the allotted time, just to enjoy it.

Sunset was beautiful that day as well and we saw a whale late in the day, swimming purposefully southwards.

"I guess I'm just a conceited little shit," said Alex after he thought again about something he had just said.

I grasped the opportunity he had given me with both hands.

"The thing I like about you, Alex," I said, "is that what you see is exactly what you get."

The only thing quainter than the mournful sound of Hans practising the banjo in the male heads was little spiky Claire spending 48 hours in there to access the washing machine and do her watch's washing.

"Close your eyes," she shouted repeatedly as she came through.

Close _our_ eyes?

We were largely naked, she had clothes on.

"Close _our_ eyes?"

21/3 - Thursday

No colour in the dawn, not like yesterday at all, but a wonderful drama of dark greys and blacks in the clouds and the texture of the sea rippling across beneath them. It made an image that Turner would have liked. I could imagine it on canvas. Cold as hell on the morning watch, minus 12 degrees Centigrade if wind chill factor allowed for. Definitely a day to start wearing my thermals.

Very good sailing – max about 30 knots of breeze from behind us, just where we want it.

Hourglass dolphins close to the boat between 0700 and 0800.

22/3 - Friday

A few more flurries of snow – water temperature down at 4 degrees Centigrade so whales seen distantly more often, also porpoises, dolphins.

More krill in cold water therefore more whales etc.

A solitary albatross this morning, an event. We seem to have left them far behind.

Morning watch very cold indeed though no wind – under engine again at this time - 0715.

Breakfast soon. I can't wait. I am eating heartily and yet still losing weight. My clothes are fallling off me and my belt is drawn in further every day.

Rolling like crazy as I write. Out of sight.

A lot of scatological back chat on deck during the watches, esp. when Alex is around. This has focused on the suggestion that Bernard farts more than the rest of us.

Why do we all fart so spectacularly on this boat? Is it the water? Last time out, I thought it was the diet, but this time the diet is normal and healthy, yet we all seem to fart more than we do on shore.

"Is that your arse?" asked Sarah bluntly last autumn when I farted and she heard it from a distance (she was the other side of the mast from me, at least ten feet away) – and it was, too, but I didn't admit it. I remember practically parting John H.'s hair with a huge fart when we were climbing the rigging and I was just in front of him. He noticed that, certainly. There was no doubt about that one at all.

And Nigel seems to have been the object of the same sort of attentions when I was climbing the companionway ladder in front of him one dark night.

Farts will happen – often involuntarily. But I do try to be away from people, to control them and to minimise their unpleasant side effects.

Bernard, on the other hand, feels that it will make him ill if he does not fart whenever he wants to – where does that idea come from? Is it especially Gallic?

Anyway, the wake up call yesterday was a little rhyme written by JP and broadcast over the tannoy. I do not recall the exact text, but the burden was that B. farts a very great deal!

I would have died of embarrassment and B. certainly felt the same (what little skin there was on view, beneath his cold-weather gear, was splendidly scarlet) – however, he loves the attention (which has continued) – for him to be laughed at is better than to be ignored.

Glen joins in some of these scatological exchanges, which is a bit embarrassing, like watching an elephant dance.

He told a story "10 cents, 20 cents, 50 cents, a dollar" which was inordinately long and not (in the end) very funny. I can't remember the punch line.

He also told one (more briefly) about a constipated accountant. "He couldn't budge it, but he worked it out with a pencil."

The schedule on this watch, the morning watch, is relentless. I thought middle watch was the worst, now I am not sure:

0330-0800 – on watch

0800-0915 – lash up and stow (clear all the hammocks), breakfast, clean teeth, morning meeting – wash?

0915-1100 – cleaning stations - two solid hours as a housemaid

1100-1200 – lecture, sail handling, man overboard or fire drills

1200-1400 – lunch + write diary

1400-1530 – ship's maintenance, painting and polishing

1600-2000 – on watch, with 20'00" for dinner and 5'00" to sling hammocks

2030 – bed

In other words, 16 straight hours of work/watch and virtually without a break – no wonder I get tired (and touchy). All this culminated last night, after 2000, with thirty minutes up the mizzen mast to furl the topsail and twenty minutes unfurling the main course.

I was shattered – too tired to get myself to bed. I am not finding much time for navigation.

Kate stepping down to the waist of the ship

Life rafts to her left, the 'fizz boat' to her right
Above, to the right, a glimpse of the pinnace

23/3 - Saturday

Bright, sharp morning with great swells, breakers, flecks of white, spume blowing up off the wave fronts as the wind reached about 40 knots. Meanwhile my foremast watch colleagues practised pushups on the quarter deck ignoring the fact that the ship was rolling through 70 or 80 degrees.

It came on to rain and sleet as all hands were called to wear ship. We are now steering something like 060 M ie NE by east.

The wind (when there is any) is from the SSW.

24/3 - Sunday - around1300

Up for 2 cold hours overnight and back into my hammock like a mole to its burrow, blindfold on, ear plugs in at 0600. I was so tired that I slept till after 1100 and missed the Sunday brunch.

Instead, I finished re-reading Patrick O'Brian's smashing book, 'Blue at the Mizzen' and I am now sitting reflecting what needs doing and what's been happening.

I am going to draft an e-mail for the children and my friends, trying to summarise it all, to sum it all up. Heaven knows when I will get to send it.

Endeavour was at 55 degrees 2 minutes south, 139 degrees 24 minutes west at 7am this morning. That means we have sailed 2,113 miles since we left Bluff, in New Zealand, and we have (only) about 3,000 to go to Cape Horn. The daily runs are averaging 130-150 miles, winds of up to 40 knots have become routine and we have set several speed records and broken them a day or two later. The best of the records is for an average of 8.01 knots over 24 hours, i.e. 192.2 nautical miles in the day. Endeavour continues to roll like a barrel going over Niagara – at least two people have suspected cracked ribs.

In the last two weeks, the ocean and the skies have often been as grey and barren and lonely and unexciting as the English Channel at its worst. The crowd of albatrosses has deserted us – we are too far south for them - but hour-glass dolphins make irregular appearances and we have glimpsed whales blowing, distantly.

Last night, in impenetrable darkness, two radar contacts suggested large icebergs within a few miles of us. The temperature on deck, allowing for the wind chill, has been below −12 Centigrade and standing watch in the bows for an hour at a time is a test of endurance and concentration. The odd large wave breaks over and it is very cold indeed, whatever you wear and however well you prepare. It is also very important to stay alert − the thought of hitting a large iceberg at speed in this vessel is very scary. We might not have much of a chance.

When I got dressed for my watch yesterday, there were 18 items in the large pile of clothes that I assembled in preparation. It looked like the contents of a sack fit for Oxfam. There are rubber sea-boots, which aren't (in my case) sea-boots at all. They are boots designed by the Milk Marketing Board of New Zealand for stockmen who stand around in cold slurry and slops all day and need a warm knee-length boot with a very good grip.

They work extremely well on deck (and cost about a third of the cost of the stylish Dubarry alternatives that all the professional crew have bought). The Captain wears the same type as I do.

Because my boots are so effective, I am only wearing one thick pair of socks − the thermal knee length socks remain in reserve, one of my secret weapons. I feel it will get seriously cold quite soon and there is no shelter at all on deck. Psychologically, it is important not to get every possible warm garment out of my locker too soon.

So I am wearing (only) underpants and thin jogging trousers under thick jogging trousers under ultra-protective heavy weather trousers and I have not yet tried out my Antarctic quality thermal long-johns (or my Antarctic quality thermal top). Their time will come, soon enough.

Above the waist, I wear a t-shirt, under an ordinary fleece under a heavy fleece under an ultra-heavy fleece under a heavy weather jacket.

Five layers. It is just about enough.

On my head, I wear a wooly hat (which the Australians call a 'beanie') under a heavy waterproof hood. I also wear the thick red scarf which Matthew gave me for Christmas. Thanks, Matt.

On top of the heavy jacket, I wear a reflective safety waistcoat and a safety harness, for when we are climbing the masts.

Is that eighteen items? I have forgotten my gloves - a potentially serious mistake when lumbering and squeezing, like Frankenstein's monster, up the constricted companion way onto the deck.

Sometimes I wear two pairs of thermal gloves, one on top of the other, under waterproof mittens, which can work well.

Otherwise, I wear thick lined gloves but still have to keep my hands in my pockets most of the time, to protect my fingers – I have under-invested in gloves (I have only got five or six pairs) but that is the only serious problem with my gear so far.

It all sounds dreadful, doesn't it? Cold, dull and wearing? But this is sailing, remember, real sailing, and of course, all I remember are the good bits:

20/3 – Wednesday

Dawn was beautiful, almost worth all the monotony of this featureless life. It has been grey and overcast but this morning the coming of the sun split the grey sky wide, streaks of pink grey and grey pink, even a band of blue up high and the glimmer of reflected sunlight on the base of rich mountains of cloud.

Sunset was beautiful that day as well and we saw a whale late in the day, swimming purposefully southwards. Next morning was quite different.

No colour in the dawn, not like yesterday at all, but a wonderful drama of dark greys and blacks and the texture of the sea rippling across a canvas that Turner would have liked.

There is always too much to do on board Endeavour. It is sometimes difficult to find the time to wash.

Could have shot a noon latitude today. It was bright enough.

Ate lunch instead.

I have had very little time for navigational exercises in the last 14 days – the watch patterns that we work are very demanding and any time free from our watches is filled with other work, which is sometimes of little utility or value, which sometimes feels as if it is imposed upon us just to keep us busy.

I would keep busy on board anyway, probably more happily and more productively, if left to my own devices. I am not exaggerating if I claim that I would have no trouble in filling three times as much free time as I can find, sometimes with projects for the benefit of everyone on board.

I am trying to find the time to write a couple of songs about Endeavour, borrowing Craig's guitar and asking Hans to accompany me on the banjo and John H. and others to sing. One of the tunes is by Buddy Holly, the other will be a version of 'The Battle of New Orleans', but with added chorus. I have only touched the guitar twice in the last six weeks and have hardly been able to mention it to Hans or John. So I am struggling a bit.

I also want to learn to serve and parcel and splice rope more effectively than I can at present. To practise, I want to make Ben, (my eldest son), a house-warming present of one of the handsome plaited rope mats which the bosun is currently having made to use as anti-chafe mats. And I want to make a padded canvas cover for my wooden sextant case – the baggage handlers at airports, who put it through the X-ray machines, are amazingly and unnecessarily rough with it and it bears the scars to prove it.

Incidentally, my birthday this time last week began with a hearty chorus of Happy Birthday over late Sunday breakfast and ended with a card from all my watch and a gift of four sticky toffees! I thought often during the day about Ben and his supposed house-warming party that night and hoped very much that he was finally established in his new house and looked forward to seeing it.

My journey on this ship, so far, totals 5,248 miles. Last year I sailed 2,226 miles on board. I am by no means the most experienced of the voyage crew, some of whom have been on board Endeavour seven or eight or more times and know her rigging backwards.

For my part, I still don't know where to find at least half of the hundreds of lines that control our sails and equipment. Sheets, tacks, halyards, bunts, clews, reefs, fancy lines and brailles, at least the names have started to make some sense, I even know (most of) their functions but where on earth are they all? Particularly in the dark, when it is very cold and you are very tired indeed, finding the right line quickly is worryingly difficult and potentially hazardous. If the wrong line is cast off by mistake, the consequences can be serious.

*****

24/3 - Sunday

Two icebergs clearly visible in daylight on the horizon, huge ones like green floating islands. Two radar echoes during the night as well.

The icebergs are real. I had hoped they were not.

We have 2,000 miles to go to reach the Cape. Time to see a lot more icebergs, hopefully not at close quarters.

I thought it was just alarmist talk, that we would be surrounded by icebergs and growlers on this leg.

At the morning meetings, Glen sometimes goes on (and on) about how cold it's going to be near the Cape, how fierce the wind and storms we will experience.

He seems to enjoy trying to frighten us (put the wind up us?)

Perhaps I was wrong to be sceptical.

Immensely, peculiarly variable, the wind and weather down here.

Bright sunshine now – sparkling waves crashing under (sometimes over) the bow. But the ship stomping along – probably at nearly 8 knots. The sky, if not blue, at least a little warmer. Temperature on deck about 4 degrees C. – windchill factor unknown but not too bad.

25/3 - Monday about 10 pm

Spooky as hell on watch – fog so thick I couldn't see the water from the stern look out position, 25 feet above the surface.

The boat moving relentlessly on like something out of The Ancient Mariner but no waves to be seen, no wind to be felt. A curious experience.

The ship's cold is with me again. Also, I have a sore foot

"Star-harrows went over our thin sleep."

George MacKayBrown − a line from his poem on the blackboard in the mess written up by John Highmore - what a beautiful set of words.

Tig, Andy, Dougal still fishing but with little success.

An albatross took Tig's lure − dead. Sad. Bad karma. A bedraggled dead or dying bird is a terrible sight on deck.

26/3 - Tuesday

Glorious bright morning − lovely visibility − we are a few miles south of the spot furthest from land in the whole world.

(Official noon position that day: 55 31 S 126 47 W)

27/3 - Wednesday

An amazingly flat calm. Most sails clewed up − proceeding under port engine. No possibility of sights at lunchtime. A very dull day indeed but (in the evening watch), we set every sail on the ship, which was enjoyable.

This morning we furled all of them again (which was not).

We are still mainly motoring and pitching like mad.

The trouble with life as voyage crew on this ship is that we are so remote from the most interesting bits of the sailing operation, ie

> 1) setting a course (studying the weather, estimating where the wind will be)
> 2) deciding on the sails to set and trimming, tending and tweaking them to optimise the performance of the ship
> 3) establishing a position and
> 4) starting again at (1)

The voyage crew really only have to do with the mechanical aspects of the ship's progress.

Daft comment. Very stupid indeed. I had signed on to be an ordinary crew member in a ship designed in the eighteenth century. And what happened in the eighteenth century navy? What did an eighteenth century crew member do? Pulled ropes, climbed masts, obeyed orders, exactly as I was doing. It was the officers (the most senior officers at that) who decided what course to steer and how much sail to employ and what methods of navigation would best serve. Daft! Perhaps I was not thinking very clearly.

29/3 - Friday

Very, very rough last night (we mustered and spent most of our watch down below, in an area called 'the Marines') – the low went off the scale, down to 970mb, with 62 knots (apparent) according to the Captain (I would have thought it was more). The wind was from the south and we could not sail against it (or even across it). We were hove to for hours drifting north.

Below decks it was (as usual) desperate, slithering and sliding all over, the ship and all its furnishings heaving underneath us. It is very wearing, very exhausting, just to live, to eat, to move around.

Oddly (given how often I have done all this) the difficulties of life at sea in really rough weather never fail to surprise me. You forget how hard it is really quickly, once it is over.

30/3 – Saturday

Captain's Rounds again - the big inspection of the week.

This week we were allocated to clean the gentlemen's quarters, in the stern, which include the Great Cabin and the Captain's quarters.

I cleaned the brass and polished the woodwork – obsessively - and told off my watchmates if they touched the polished surfaces after I'd finished with them.

Kate mustered her best school psychology qualifications and announced that I have an obsessive/compulsive disorder but I think I just like doing a reasonably thorough job and not having my watchmates mess it up before it's even been inspected.

Heading north of east now with a westerly and variable wind 11-25 knots - we should be heading much further south but we can't.

Milo Rocks! (wrote little spiky Claire in her notebook - what is Milo, a milky drink?)

All girls are scrunchers! (Kate, investigating the lavatory paper habits of her watchmates – but Glen scrunches too.)

Alex and Nigel left a yellow plastic duck floating in the bowl in the heads for the Captain's inspection. Even the Captain was taken by surprise and Glen was in fits.

Nat and Geo were filming at the time.

Kate has been enthusiastically (and not very discreetly) involved with Tig for some weeks now. There is evidently a sexual dimension to the time they spend together or, to put it less coyly, they are fucking as often as they possibly can (and why not?).

It has become Alex's practise to pour scorn on the idlers (amongst whom Tig is numbered).

Kate, naturally, resents this.

"Idlers are cool, don't fuck with the idlers," she said, this afternoon, to try to shut Alex up.

Then she realised what she'd said (and so did we).

A lot of laughter followed. It was a classic moment and she blushed scarlet, which suited her enormously.

Perhaps she should follow her own advice.

Clare has been Watchleader this week and has done very well. She explains everything, speaks clearly and <u>asks</u> us to do things instead of telling us.

Morale has improved enormously in the last two weeks. We're having a lot of fun again, an awful lot of jokes (we are known for it). Many are scatological, few worth writing down – but attempts to list all the possible slang expressions for 'penis' produced the rather wonderful expression "crimson crowbar", which I had not heard before. We also squawk like penguins when leaving the deck at midnight (we are nothing if not inconsiderate).

Alex pretending to be a penguin laying an egg had to be heard to be believed. Foremast watch is a very joyful gang of people to which to belong.

Clare was asked how she was getting on with the animals (meaning her watch - us).

She and a few others started to speculate on what animals each of us could be.

They told me that I ended up being compared to a rhinoceros and I asked them why. I was rather flattered by the answer which said that they defined me as 'apparently placid but can run very fast if necessary .... largely solitary but capable of being sociable' to which I added (mentally) 'dangerous if crossed.'

At least they have me down as one of the big beasts of this jungle – that re-assures me!

(Why do I need to be re-assured?)

The young people have started pairing off, or thinking about it. Kate and Tig sit side by side together. They have been able to satisfy and formalise their sexual feelings for each other. Regularly.

Craig and Jennaya sit opposite. Her hands reach for him more often than his for her. Alex, muted at last, gazes at Tiffany as if he were capable of being serious (perhaps he is, with her). Sometimes he rests his head in her lap (lucky head) and she looks even more like a Madonna than usual and he like the broken Christ.

Clare seems to have no suitor or lover, at least yet. She is sadly serious about her life sometimes. I would like to see her swept off her feet, learning abandonment. I think she misses that (and may never, ever, discover it.)

How wrong I was, about Clare!

31/3 - Sunday - easter Sunday

I have kept the tiny easter card, which, with a few miniature chocolate eggs, Fleur and Camilla presented me with when I was going on watch today. It meant a lot at the time – it was like a sort of affirmation, almost a permanent or lasting hug or gentle kiss, and I got one of those as well.

Affection is something I crave out here, though there is a lot of friendship.

I wrote another draft e-mail for my family and friends, to send whenever I can:

Sunday 31st. March

Endeavour was at 55 degrees 43 minutes south, 115 degrees 19 minutes west at noon yesterday. We have sailed 3023 miles since we left Bluff, in New Zealand, and we have about 1,500 to go to Cape Horn (and 11,000 to Whitby.)

The daily runs this week have been as little as 68.5 miles and as much as 169.5. Our progress is dominated and often interrupted by the erratic and changeable weather. Low pressure systems sweep up astern of us and usually give us high winds and big seas and push us forward. High pressure systems dominate when the lows pass but they give us calm or quiet conditions.

We are using our one remaining engine quite regularly when the ship's speed through the water drops below about three knots. Between noon on 27/3 and noon on 28/3, we did not sail at all but covered 115 miles at an average of 4.7 knots under power alone.

We have seen no more icebergs or whales this week and it has not been vilely cold but cold in a normal, civilized way so that our teeth chatter only gently and most of our extremities remain detectable.

I am still not wearing my thermal underwear and socks, but I am thinking seriously about them.

Once I put them on, I have nothing left in reserve.

The wind was heavy on Thursday and the seas were huge – more than thirty feet and breaking close to us. The ship was heaving and pitching violently and it was so dangerous on deck that we mustered and spent our watch in the cramped area called 'the Marines', down below.

Only three members of the watch (two on the helm and one on bow watch, by the starboard cannon) were exposed outside to the elements at any one time. We were hove to and drifted northwards for many hours, with an easterly gusting at more than 70 knots in our teeth.

That storm was an impressive, awe-inspiring sight. I won't forget it. But last night, sailing with almost all available sails set in winds from 19-40 knots, was even better.

The ship roared along, in roughly the right direction, with rather too much sail set, healing determinedly to port and pushing gallons of white water to each side, waves breaking under her bluff, aggressive bows, twenty foot surfing waves rolling past her hull as if they were playing with us.

The wind was on the starboard quarter and there was lots of it.

When the moon came out from behind the broken clouds, it lit up the water like a pathway to another universe.

"It just can't get any fucking better," said Nigel Longster, one of my watchmates, shaking his head at the moonshine. "You could read a book by this."

A few of the stars showed themselves.

Alpha and Beta Centauri clearly pointed to the Southern Cross before we could see it, then the Cross itself glimmered through the clouds, a pointer in the sky.

"My favourite constellation," said Nigel, looking up. "My favourite fucking constellation."

One of the stay sails started flapping and the lead helmsman called for more starboard helm to bring the ship back up to the wind.

"Seven to starboard. Quickly!"

The helmsmen were panting as they heaved the wheel around.

"Seven to starboard. On!" said the helmsman's mate and he relaxed.

"You think it's good," said Nigel with something like joy in his voice. "You think it's so fucking good."

He paused.

"And then it gets fucking better."

Nigel Longster was one of the gang going all the way to Whitby. He's a very likeable, much bearded New Zealander, who lives in Queensland, in Australia and rides a Harley Davidson and keeps bull terriers and works in a brewery and is covered all over with tattoos.

His father went to sea from Whitby and ended up in New Zealand and settled there. His grandfather and eight uncles, his father's brothers, all went to sea as well. He expects quite a reception in Staithes, just north of Whitby, where many of his relatives still live.

Nigel looks gruff or even grumpy. His heavy beard hides his mouth and reaches up towards his eyes. But he laughs a lot. His smile is very kind. The young women on board seem to adore him.

If he is suggestive (and he is) it is always with a smile and laughter – backed by honest admiration. He hides a kind heart behind a very grumpy beard.

On board Endeavour, the space in your locker is all the space you own and entirely control. It is very precious.

Your locker is like a little island inside a cupboard where your personality hides and resides and where you can be yourself. It's the one place where the routines and the rules of the ship can't reach you.

If my locker were big enough, I would sleep inside it sometimes, just to get away from everyone.

This week, I have been having trouble with my locker, which is disastrous.

Seawater has been leaking in, because of the very rough weather. My locker contains almost everything I brought with me – important and relatively valuable things like my sextant and my big camera; things of personal importance like my notebooks, good luck cards, memorabilia and money; books I want to read; all my clean clothes, underpants, dry socks and reserve sweaters. Also, my precious pristine thermal underwear.

At the morning meeting on Friday, I drew the attention of the Chief Officer to the fact that my locker was leaking.

"All wooden ships leak," he said, and passed on to other topics.

I am uncertain what to do next. But I have wrapped everything possible in plastic bags.

1/4 - Monday

'Mizzling' as in mizzling rain – drizzle? An expression used by Captain Marryat in Mr. Midshipman Easy, a childhood book which I have just re-read with much enjoyment.

What a lovely adjective!

2/4 - Tuesday 0855

Miserable conditions, calm, heavy overcast, mizzling rain, barometer falling like a stone. Tetchy today. Middle Watch starting to bite again? Sleep deprivation kicking in again?

Endurance, that's it. Endurance, survival, self-abnegation. Strength though denial.

My mother died ten years ago today – and I only remembered, three quarters of the way through the morning meeting. She would like to see me here and to know about it but I am glad she is no longer alone, without my father's company and presence. She missed him terribly, her last three years.

3/4 - Wednesday

After the sad monotony of yesterday, two watches full of incident, excitement and beauty.

On middle watch, in near darkness, the mad arc of the mainmast curved down towards the sea through a sky brindled with dim moonlight above a sea spewing with violence.

A wave travelled the quarterdeck at head height, caught us all by surprise; my clothes are still wet from it 12 hrs. later (nothing will dry – our mess deck is awash as well as the lavatories).

Some gusts of wind were more than 45 knots. It snowed this morning, stinging the face and naked hands, streaming horizontally across the windswept decks.

This afternoon, the sun is bright and small rainbows form in the spray by the blustering bow. Alex and Craig whoop when a big wave hits. Even I smile or laugh when I see it.

The seascape is a meadow of beauty, the waves gallop through it like wild horses, tossing their white bright manes.

Snapshots in my head:

Rushing onto the deck in the great storm just as the bow of the boat pitched precipitously down the front of a great wave and into the chasm behind. The angle of pitch, fore and aft? 50 or 60 degrees? I could barely stay on my feet.

Another snapshot:

The crazy geometry of the furled mizzen topsail, crojack brace and mizzen course, silhouetted against the magic billows of the main course and main topsail as the two masts swing like mad fishing rods across the glimmer and glitter of the fierce sky and the torrential sea from starboard to port and the driving waves speed noisily beneath the hull.

A final snapshot:

Craig, when he spotted the killer whales bombing towards us, arms wide, knees bent, thumbs up, a great smile, dark glasses.

"Yes!"

Jubilance in every gesture.

4/4 - Thursday

Very cold on the eighteenth century deck this morning.

"This journey brought to you by the words 'fucking' and 'cold'," muttered Alex, shivering.

"Take me back to Queensland," said Nigel, who stayed in his hammock till the last possible moment.

"I'll be on the same bus," said the Captain later at breakfast.

Chris Blake likes the hot weather too – don't we all?

Barometric Pressure very very low at 972. Storm force winds expected.

Wind now from the south – up to 62-65 knots (apparent), more than 70 true. Running north with it behind us.

Turning up to reach across it (and make a better course) carries too much risk of broaching.

I finally saw Captain Blake lose his balance on deck – it's taken 8,000 miles, but I got the photograph.

A moment later, a wave broke above me, on the sail above my head and I got soaked - so did the camera. Not very clever.

My little Minox was never the same again. My children bought me another one (of the same vintage) for my sixtieth birthday.

5/4 - Friday

Routine day yesterday – mizzling and cold in the afternoon, the same at midnight (we were down in the Marines again).

On the helm in the last hour of Middle Watch, the wind built steadily towards 40 and 45 and the ship howled along with everything set except the mizzen mast sails.

She continued to sail like that when we went down to sleep but all hands were called up during breakfast to hand or furl the topsails and get control again – the wind was over 60 knots and the seas were marvellous to watch – fascinating and startling, sparkling with light and life.

"Oh, que c'est apre, que c'est dur."

Persephone? Stravinsky?

(How harsh it is, how hard)

Svetlana Beriosova read the narration in the recording that I remember.

I met her, once or twice, when Zoe Dominic and I were working on our book about Frederick Ashton. Zoe knew her well and she was a wonderful dancer, in her prime, particularly in Giselle.

Good to remember the warmth and luxury and the beauty of the Royal Opera House, where I once spent so much time.

Especially out here.

5/4 – Friday (continued)

The whole day has seen us hurtling NE (not the direction we want) in great style (staysails and forecourse only) – I was on the helm and it was very invigorating but I have no idea what speed we were doing. The waves were about 20-25 feet, the wind up to 45 knots and more.

Rough and wild seas – treacherous underfoot.

Fell twice yesterday – once spectacularly on the quarterdeck, flat on my front over the tiller, sliding towards the scuppers, the second landing in the box of sea boots at the top of the stairs down to the galley. A few more bruises in unexpected places, a nasty twinge in my left knee, which I seem to have twisted.

I was lucky to get away with the first fall - it was by far the worst yet.

196 degrees true (wind) – the first time a storm has gone on for more than 24 hours.

The sun shone brightly for most of the day but I wouldn't risk my sextant on deck to take a reading.

6/4 - Saturday 0845

Great middle watch 40-50 knots steering 110-120 on the wind. Helming about 400 tons of ship at 7 or more knots (teamed up with Kate and Bernard) was an excellent experience. What a privilege! What a WONDERFUL ship!

Verses for my new Cape Horn song:

> *It's dark tonight, the Horn's still not in sight*
> *the waves are huge, the sea's all white*

6/4 - Saturday

Afternoon watch was spectacular. The ocean is very lively. Bernard and I had volunteered to relieve the galley crew and make lunch tomorrow but I think the the Captain think it's a bit too rough for the two of us to gobble about in the galley all day Sunday so I will get my lay day rest (which I badly need.) I am quite relieved. I was going to make 'bigos', which is a hunter's stew from Poland. Mixed meats and mushrooms, loads of garlic and red wine.

Very nice indeed - but in these conditions? Could have been testing. And I am tired again. Terribly tired.

7/4 - Sunday

Writing this on middle watch at about 0140 – I am in the nav. room watching the radar. The seas build and build as the storm continues (three days now) – windspeed 30-50, all from the SE and the ship rolls horribly. It is difficult to sleep, even in a hammock. Then, when you are very tired, it is difficult to do ordinary things, to make tea, to get dressed, to move about safely, to sling your hammock.

JP fell out of his hammock and hurt himself a lot (he had not tied it on properly but, as he pointed out, what does he know about knots? He is a computer whizz. He should have been shown how to do it at one of the introductory sessions but I wonder if he was - we left Fremantle in such a hurry, perhaps there were no introductory sessions). Tig and Ally fell heavily as well and they are young and fit and professional and should be able to look after themselves.

I have been quite lucky so far, and careful. I haven't hurt myself badly.

8/4 - Monday

Famous last words?

I fell down the companion way into the twentieth century mess this morning – in front of 90% of the crew. Only dignity suffered. My own fault, too. Those leather shoelaces on my boat shoes again. Must tie them properly, make sure they're shorter. Otherwise the ends get under your feet and you slither about on them, it's like being on roller skates.

Overcast today – no sights (again) Storm passed, the Cape Horn song almost completed.

> *The albatrosses swoop and soar*
> *The whales sneak past – wish we'd seen more*

8/4 - Monday (continued) around 2100

Lay day very welcome yesterday and Alex no longer the watchleader – glad about that. I didn't like having to argue with him or ask anything of him.

Routine day – now on morning watch, 0400-0800, 1600-2000.

With additional sail-handling, tonight, (we've just finished) that amounts to seventeen and a half hours without a proper break.

All the watches are bad, but I think morning watch is probably the most exhausting.

However, I skived off this afternoon – instead of helping with maintenance, I learned to operate Martin's video camera.

Trivial Pursuit this evening.

It infuriates me.

If you can answer the questions, they're banal, if you can't they're humiliating.

Mark you, it helps if you are winning (and we weren't). You don't feel so bad about it then!

In the army and in prison, the first thing to happen is that the conscript or inmate is allocated a number and loses control of most or all of his or her private possessions and timetable.

How curious – the same things happen on Endeavour. I am number four in foremast watch. I identify myself in this way at least four times per day, at the beginning and end of each watch and sometimes in between. Does it de-personalise you? Do you lose a little bit of your identity each time you call the number instead of answering to your name?

In a curious sort of way, neither personality nor achievments matter much out here. As I wrote before, it is simply a question of whether you can cope. Can you look after yourself and your clothes on board, keep yourself clean and fed, get enough sleep, turn up punctually on watch, climb the masts or haul the halyards when you need to.

Can you hack it?

It should be the Endeavour's motto.

Interesting to reflect that a 19 year old like Kate may never normally take responsibility for her own wardrobe, schedule, routine etc. Kate's been on Endeavour before but she still manages to be late on watch occasionally and I lend her my torch sometimes, when we're kitting up, because she's always lost or mislaid some item of apparel or equipment.

Spoke to one of the officers the other day − I claimed that one bad day, on passage, would be pretty normal for me, one bad day on a long passage, when I really didn't think I wanted to be out there.

She thought that was a good average. (So do I).

On this trip, it would be more like one bad day in four.

Pete the Fish new watchleader − good!

They all do one week each - Kate's next, I think - and I have declined to do it.

I used to spend a lot of time managing people and taking responsibility for them. That is not what I am out here to do now, rather the opposite.

9/4 – Tues. 1205

Mizzling rain again – grey overcast – horrible!

No sights poss. Calmish. Magnetic course 080

Haven't climbed for ages – climbed twice today (main course unreefed, mizzen topsail furled) – can't say I liked it esp. in pouring rain (main) or pitch dark (mizzen top). However, I can do it.

Also got stuck on the helm as the helsman's assistant, 'the muscles' for nearly three hours .... not happy with that – Pete the Fish seemed to have forgotten I was there!

10/4 - Wednesday

Pete's first suggestion this morning was that I should go back on the helm as 'muscles'.

I declined, so he put me on as 'brains' (the main helmsman) instead – just as tiring but a lot more stimulating ....

44,000 containers per year fall overboard! Wow! Obviously, most of them sink. But it would be possible, even in Endeavour, to get completely wiped out if you hit a floating container at speed. In the middle of the Indian Ocean, Dan and I were gliding along in our tiny (steel) boat in smooth seas with a light breeze on our quarter when there was suddenly a distinct heavy thump at the bow and a grinding noise along our starboard side. We rushed on deck.

A large log - the bottom half of a big mango tree - was drifting out behind us.

We had hit it fair and square, despite the vast expanses of water which surrounded us. (We were more than a thousand miles from land in any direction.)

Fortunately, the sea was calm, the wind was slight. We hit it nice and slowly.

But if we had been tearing along in a big wind, surfing down the front of a wave at 12 or 13 knots, that log could have made a severe impression even on a metal hulled boat and might have holed and sunk a glass fibre yacht.

The tree stump was about 6 feet by 8 feet in section (48 square feet) and the area of our bow was about 3 feet by 7 feet (21 square feet).

How these two small surfaces managed to find each other and to make contact is still a mystery to me. The chances of it happening seem so very remote.

More verses of the song, particularly:

> *It's morning now, the sea is blue*
> *the storm's blown through and the world is new*

I wonder who can sing it for me? Lucy was so terrific last time, in 2001. I need to find someone like her. Later I proposed to Tiffany that she should sing it − a resounding lack of enthusiasm ensued.

10/4 - Wednesday (continued)

Oh dear! Heading west! (and a little north) - quite the wrong direction!

We approached the Chilean coast, close enough to spot the loom of a lighthouse beam from one of the Evangelista Islands but the wind remained obstinately in the south with a little east in it as well − exactly the direction in which we have to go to get round the Horn.

Rather than be trapped on a lee shore, we wore ship and turned away (heading, the Captain told us in joke, directly for Tahiti).

We may spend days to-ing and fro-ing like this, but I hope not. Everyone has the Channels already, cabin fever – they have all been anticipating the landfalls, at the Horn and Port Stanley, since the day we left Bluff.

Also, food is running short. No fruit now for days and days – no more biscuits on night watch.

A poem, not a song:

> *The west wind strokes the seas and kisses skies*
> *As I would like to stroke a woman's thighs*
> *Gently and often, lovingly and bold,*
> *Inflamed, enraptured, passionate - and cold*

(Another six lines written and in notebook – could make a sonnet? But I think the extra lines weaken it rather than add to it. Maybe I will look at it again sometime.)

> *This wind will stroke the sea and kiss the sky*
> *When woman, thighs and I in earth will lie*

(And not together, more's the pity!)

11/4 - Thursday

Overcast, barometric pressure rising, south wind – tried wearing at 0845 when the wind seemed to be veering – however, the best poss. course we could achieve afterwards was 070 M, to the north of east, ie No Bloody Good.

We wore back, promptly and are still heading west with no windshift likely.

12/4 - Friday - 1430

52 38 S – 76 45 W

Two days ago we were further south and west than this (53 20S 75 32 W) – we have made no progress at all and our current course is 89-93 True, which will take us into the Straits of Magellan but not round the Horn. It is still completely overcast and we are now less than 70 miles off Desolation Island in the Archipelago Reina Adelaida in about 400-1555 fathoms, with no hope of finding soundings before we hit the rocks.

We would be in grave danger with only dead reckoning and my sextant to guide us. (We haven't seen the sun for days and days). How would I play it, if I were the only navigator and there was no GPS on board?

13/4 - Saturday – 0635

Thick overcast – viz down to 1-1.5 miles. Course about 150M, variation 16-18 east. So we are making south, as we want, at 6-7 knots over the ground with a Force 4-5 breeze on our starboard quarter.

Stood by at noon, with Gerald, to try for a noon sight – but the sun was completely concealed, there was no point in even bringing the sextant up on deck.

By accident, just this morning, I came across an article by Skip Novak about navigating the second Whitbread Round the World Race in 1977.

The article was a print out from his web-site which is called www.pelagic.co.uk

He describes approaching Cape Horn from the west as we are doing, in overcast conditions. He sees a break in the clouds, grabs a sun-sight, comps it. Two hours later, another break in the clouds, another observation, another set of calculations.

He crosses the two position lines (which have only a 30 degree angle of cut) and deduces from this scanty evidence that his estimated latitude is spot on and that the vessel is (jubilantly) 40 miles further down their track (ie nearer the Horn) than his DR had implied. "We were ten miles north of our supposed track and a healthy forty miles ahead of schedule."

If your actual position is ahead of your **DR**, you are in great danger if the skies are overcast and you are running down onto a lee shore. Also, two position lines with only two hours between them are not much by way of hard evidence.

You have to have a lot of balls to navigate that way – but, of course, at that time, there was no alternative. You either navigated on the edge or you stayed at home.

14/4 Sunday

On the bow by myself early this morning. Delightful. Thrilling. The ship is so beautiful. In detail as well as in outline, in close up as well as in long shot.

I looked at it and loved it, suddenly, with different eyes - observing things I had seen many times with fresh perception.

I wrote this in my notebook on deck. My fingers got very very cold very quickly. Otherwise, I would have written more:

> *Everything on the deck around me is functional, hand-crafted, beautifully appropriate and much-handled, worn and scarred with constant use.*

> *This is a living, working museum-piece, which we inhabit and use. I feel very content and fortunate – even the noise of the waves is muted and soothing.*

How little I write about sounds and smells in these journals. Nothing about the food either. Curious omissions?

Everyone else who writes about sailing mentions the noise of the wind in the rigging, especially in stormy conditions.

But I was not very conscious of it, either because I was deafened by all the garments I wore on my head to keep myself warm or (more likely?) that my nearly sixty year old hearing apparatus minimised the high frequency sounds, the whistling and howling sounds, that surround me.

I must ask a younger crew member, Craig, perhaps, about the sounds and how he remembers them.

As for smell - there must have been a variety of strong odours on the eighteenth century deck where we all slept and worked and lived.

The hatch to the deck had to be closed for most of our time crossing the Pacific. A stranger would undoubtedly have sniffed disbelievingly, if suddenly finding him or her self in our midst. Socks, feet, trainers, underwear, damp clothes, sleeping bags, intestinal emissions (farts) ...... not to speak of the smell of the sail cloth, the warps, the equipment and stores of tar and varnish with which we also shared the space.

And yet I do not remember the smells and I make no comments about them at all, in any of the notebooks.

I suppose I just got used to them.

0738

Wallowing in a light southerly a few miles off Gilbert Island, Stewart Island and Londonderry Island. About 40 miles off shore. We might see the nearest peak (8,000 feet) a little later. Cape Horn is within reach now – perhaps 150 miles away. It is bitterly cold and horribly calm. Barometric pressure (BP) is steady or rising.

We are going to make it.

*****

HEAVY WEATHER

I went on deck in a hurry, wearing heavy duty thermal underwear and everything else I could manage. I wore three pairs of gloves and, on my head, a balaklava helmet underneath a woollen hat underneath the heavy waterproof hood of my Antarctic oilskins.

I counted once, when we were in the Southern Ocean, and found that I was wearing a total of 21 different garments, counting pairs of socks and boots and gloves as single items.

We had waves thirty five foot high rolling the ship from side to side as if she were a barrel going down Niagara Falls. We needed to shorten sail urgently. The temperature was about -20 degrees Centigrade because of the wind chill.

That night, the wind was gusting above fifty knots as I started to climb the shrouds which hold up the main mast of the bark called Endeavour. I was clumsy and slow. I felt old. I had too many clothes on. I was too hot.

I wondered, not for the first time - what on earth made me want to do this? Why ever did I come out here? How did my life change so much?

Our task was to take in and furl the biggest sail on board and we had done it many times before. But, that night, the conditions were extreme. It was dark, it was very rough, it was frightening and dangerous - much more dangerous than usual. About fourteen of us were involved - most of my own foremast watch and some of the group called 'the idlers', members of the professional crew who work very hard (they're not idle at all) but who don't stand watches every day; they are called up on deck only in emergency, when things get tough, because they are good sailors, good workers, and fit and young.

I was 59 years old at that time. I had spent most of my life in sedentary occupations, producing and directing radio and television programmes, writing scripts and plays and novels, running a restaurant, helping people with IT problems.

I had always been the boss of all my enterprises and now I was just another ordinary crew member on Endeavour, at everyone's beck and call, liable to be summoned to furl or set sail at any time of the day or night.

I have always valued my privacy and my solitude above everything.

On Endeavour, I had to sling my hammock in 14 inches of space on the main deck with 30 other people.

I had always disliked heights and now I was climbing the main mast of a square rigger in gale force winds.

What on earth happened, to change my life into this? Who or what inspired me to do something so demanding and so seemingly masochistic and so life-enhancing and special?

It was pitch black that night. I had taken off my glasses because it was raining as well as blowing. I had got used to working largely by feel when it was dark or when it rained, when things were difficult and I wouldn't be able see through my glasses.

I climbed the shrouds, the standing rigging, without any major problems. I had done it lots of time before and we were on the windward side, which meant the wind was behind us. There's no safety line when you are climbing - you could fall off, onto the deck or into the sea quite easily but we were being blown <u>on</u> to the shrouds, which are like tarred manilla rope ladders and, because we were going to work on the main sail, we didn't have to struggle up past the overhang of what are called the futtock shrouds, to reach the fighting top and climb higher and deal with the topsail.

All we had to do was to leave the safety of the mast, step out on to the main yard, on to the foot rope, and clip our waist belt on to the line on top of the yard itself.

Then we could get to work in reasonable confidence, knowing that we were attached to something strong, that the cold wind swirling energetically about us would not carry us away, that even if the sail blew up at us and knocked us off the foot rope, we wouldn't fall far or hurt ourselves seriously.

That is the theory, at any rate.

In fact, for a tall, heavy man like me to fall even a few feet off the main yard in a big wind and a big sea would have been very very uncomfortable, potentially life-threatening, terrifying. The waist belt would probably ride up over your ribs and might break one or two. You'd be wrenched and twisted by the wind in all sorts of unexpected directions. Flailing around to get yourself back onto a secure footing would be a major struggle and climbing down again could be a big problem. The shock effect of even a small fall would be huge.

That night, my own safety was a priority. I wanted to do the work, to get the sail in (fast!) but my own survival was what I thought about first. When you are my age, you know that you can die, that you can hurt yourself. When you are young, like Eric Newby writing about his experiences in 'The Last Great Grain Race', or Richard Dana writing about life at sea in 'Two Years Before the Mast', you do anything aloft or on shore without thinking how dangerous it is, because you don't understand risk - you don't feel that you are vulnerable, in fact you are sure that you will live forever.

That feeling passes, once you are about forty or when your joints start to creak a little and you get long-sighted and can't read the newspaper without glasses because your arms aren't long enough.

That night, I had to step out onto the footrope of the main yard from the relative security of the main mast. It should have been easy. I had done it lots of times before.

Pete the Fish, a professional sailor from New Zealand, was in front of me, and he did it. Bernard, who is a waiter, born in France but now living in Sydney in Australia, was in front of me and he did it. I got to the stepping off point and gasped and froze completely. The yard wasn't square, wasn't braced at the usual 90 degrees angle to the mast. It was at an oblique angle instead, and that meant that on the port side, where I was, it seemed that the 'step' I was supposed to take was seven or eight feet long.

We were 50 or 60 feet up and the boat was rolling and the wind was howling and the waves were sending spume and foam almost up to our level. There was a whole gang of people behind me, wondering why I had stopped moving forward.

I looked at the yard and I tried to swing around the back of the rigging to find a platform which would bring me closer to it and allow me to step on to it.

I couldn't understand how the guys in front had made it on to the yard at all. I couldn't crack it. Either because I didn't have my glasses on or because the people in front were much more limber than me, I could not get on the yard on that side, on that night.

I climbed round to the starboard side instead, not without difficulty under those conditions, because then the wind was trying to pluck me off the ship and the roll of the ship was heavier in that direction so again survival was the name of the game. But the step onto the yard was much shorter there, just a couple of feet, and I got out onto the foot rope and clipped on and started to help, thinking all the time of my own safety as well as what I was doing, making sure that I was as secure as you can be in a gale force wind up the mast of a ship rolling through more than ninety degrees. "One hand for the ship," goes the saying, "and one for yourself."

Or, as Dana wrote in the nineteenth century about a stormy night near Cape Horn when he did the same job as me:

"That night we had need of every finger that God gave us."

Elsewhere, he refers to a ship-mate:

"He was a true sailor, every finger a fish-hook."

On Endeavour, we needed all our fishhook-fingers and even our eyelashes just to hold on, to protect ourselves, that night and the work was very slow, but we got the sail in eventually and made a reasonable job of it - the furl looked quite respectable in the morning, in the light of next day's dawn. There were no big bundles, like dead cows, hiding under the canvas 'skin' on the outside of the neatly rolled up sail.

That was the heaviest work I ever did on board Endeavour.

That was the night I feared for my life.

*****

14/4 - Sunday

No sights possible today.

GPS noon position: 55 41 S, 72 20 W.

5053.7 miles since Bluff.

Fremantle to Hobart = 2114 miles
Hobart to Bluff = 1021 miles

Cairns to Bali (2001) was 2026 miles (I think).

So I have now sailed more than 10,000 miles on board Endeavour!

And I still don't know where all the lines are .... I still don't know the ropes.

I wonder if I ever will?

15/4 - Monday

Land at last – the uninhabited Diego Ramirez islands, 50 miles SW of Cape Horn.

Who was Diego Ramirez? Must look him up. Portugese navigator? Sixteenth/seventeenth century?

Diego Ramirez de Arellano was the 'cosmografo', which I take to mean navigator and map-maker, of an expedition led by Bartolome and Gonzalo Garcia del Nodal and they discovered the islands named after him in 1619.

What on earth were they doing in the area? The King of Spain had sent them to explore the possibility of getting round Cape Horn and into the Pacific. They managed it, too. These were, at that time, the most southerly islands ever discovered and remained so until Cook's second voyage took him even further south and he discovered the South Sandwich Islands 150 years later.

Fierce and jagged – utterly desolate. We sailed straight through two of them, between them – partly, perhaps, to give Nat and Geo the best possible shot.

A young seal swam out to have a look at us. Inquisitive, of course .... they all are. A very grey, bleak, calm morning.

Sometimes being on Endeavour is like being a child again. You have no real responsibilities, almost no need to think for yourself. It is sometimes quite a disadvantage if you do try to think for yourself and do things your way (instead of the Endeavour way).

There is also the continual dressing and un-dressing and what a struggle that can be - just like when you were a toddler.

INFANITLISM (sic) I wrote in my notebook - in capitals:

"arms stuck in jackets, the wrong foot in the right boot – almost tears of frustration."

16/4 – Tuesday - dawn, at Cape Horn

I can not believe it. We are there at last. I cried.

Mackerel sky with blue – the best sunrise ever over Cape Horn, which was gentler, more like a mountain than I expected and much less desolate.

We were only two or three miles away. We saw it clearly.

The guys have been like schoolkids on an outing – now they've found the sweet shop.

Gentle breeze – due aft (westerly at last). The crew broke out the stun'sls, the fair weather sails, and thought of rigging them.

Scottish Graeme was in his shorts again, because he'd promised or bet someone he would go round Cape Horn in his britches.

Someone tells me that Cape Horners are entitled to have a pig tattoed on the calf of their right leg and to wear a gold earring in their left ear and to piss into the wind, which they have clearly conquered.

"The Horn's putting on a show," said Joe the mud-doctor to my right. He was wearing his charity shop tail coat over boxer shorts. It was around dawn. He looked like a demented, very tired, penguin.

We were all slightly mad that morning. It was, for every single one of us, the culmination of a lifetime's hopes and aspirations.

To taste real adventure, to sail somewhere special, to fulfil ourselves, to find out what it all really meant, being alive, risking disappointment, making it at last.

It was our own very special spectacular. Even as I was writing, the sky started to cloud over. Later, the wind hit us hard - up to Force 11 - and, in the next twenty four hours, we sailed the most nautical miles in a day that Endeavour has ever achieved - 202 miles in 24 hours - hot shit!

Screaming along.

Before that, as we drifted past the legendary place in balmy sunshine, I sketched the outline of the Horn in my notebook − twice − and I never sketch anything, because I am so bad at it.

16/4 – Tuesday - noon, at Cape Horn

A great day – with a drop of fizzy wine to celebrate and a very genuine party mood.

The Captain produced souvenir tee shirts for us all – a million pictures were snapped and swapped.

Jane, Kate and Tiff at Cape Horn

We formally passed the crucial longitude (67 degrees 16 minutes W) at 09 20 exactly but by 1030 or 1100 it was like New Year's day or late on Christmas Day, "oh, that was fun, that was special, what do we do now?"

So we cleaned the Captain's cabin and double reefed and set the main topsail and I tried for a noon shot with my sextant and wrote the final verses for my song.

Oh, what a day, what a scene!
Oh what a place to have been!

Cape Horn at dawn - 16th. April, 2002

I cannot do justice to it. Ten years later, thinking back on it, revising what I wrote, I still cannot do justice to it. Almost nothing in my life has meant so much as seeing Cape Horn at close quarters and sailing slowly round it on that wonderful ship, with those very special people after all the delays, the expectations, the frustrations and the privations - there we were, on that morning, on that day, with the sun rising above the peninsula which is Cape Horn and filling the sky with beauty.

Magic.

I hope I remember it until the very moment when I die.

I think I will.

17/4 – Wednesday - 1700

Today has been such a contrast with our passage round the Horn. When we went on watch this morning, the conditions were superbly, arrogantly, heedlessly stormy, with gusts during the forenoon watch logged at 48 knots. It felt like more. The sea was wonderful and terrible and would have been terrifying, in any other vessel. Endeavour is so sturdy and so seaworthy that she makes everyone complacent about the strong winds and wicked rollers out here. Rough conditions are greeted with whoops of joys and the kids enjoy it all as if it were an entertainment (which, of course, it is – I could watch the sea in this mood for days and days and wrestling with the helm can be stimulating as well as exhausting.)

I can't help thinking that I would like to see some of these kids frightened – just for a moment. It might make them careful.

I'm not sure I want to be out here when it happens.

Endeavour at full tilt in the Southern Ocean

Coils of line falling off the cleats - the helmsmen hanging on for grim death - it was like this for days at a time. We rolled through at least 100 degrees and pitched through 50.

18/4 – Thursday

Beautiful, beautiful day – bright sun, sea full of whitecaps, 30 knots of breeze. We set a day run record yesterday – 202 nautical miles – and we'll be in the Falklands tomorrow morning. Land at last.

What on earth will it be like?

Violent hailstorm around 1530 – fun and games with hailballs on the amazingly slippery deck. Heaven help a sailor reefing and furling in conditions like that. It would be lethal. So were the hail-ball throwers – I retreated promptly. Even toting and using Martin's video camera was no protection. Kate got me with a good one. "That's fucking stupid," I said angrily, though it had done me no harm and the camera was dry.

I always get it wrong with Kate.

19/4 – Friday

A handwritten sign greeted us in Stanley:

WELCOME, TO THIS SIDE OF THE HORN
FROM THE FAR SIDE OF THE WORLD

A gift from Peter Weir, the film-maker, who also sent us a very large cake.

It was good to be back on shore.

We went for a drink and the pub didn't rock from side to side and our glasses didn't crash to the floor if we forgot to hold on to them.

That was a genuine surprise, a revelation!

It took a while to get used to standing still.

I left the pub sober(ish) and went back to the ship and cleaned up and headed for my hammock and found Jennaya writing a letter to the father who abandoned her when she was tiny, when her mother died, and I talked to her about fathers who have to abandon daughters and the guilt they feel and how best (or how least badly) to engage.

"Send him postcards," I said. "Not letters. Letters need a response. They make you feel guilty if you don't write back. Postcards aren't like that."

So I think she is writing him a postcard or two and I think that for a moment or two, I made a difference to her life, perhaps I helped her, perhaps it helped that I told her about failure, weakness and the sadnesses of life and how difficult it can sometimes be to love and how fathers sometimes come to stay away from small daughters, as I did myself, when my daughter Claudia was very young because I couldn't confront or bear to be reminded of my own horrible guilt, not at having fathered her but at having brought pain to my wife - who was not my daughter's mother.

21/4 – Sunday

Gangplank duty between 0200 and 0300 – enlivened by the Captain, carousing in his sarong and furry boots in the Great Cabin and venturing forth onto the quay to souvenir the handwritten banner (10 ft. by 6ft.) on the side of the shed. "Don't be so fucking intelligent," he roared at me when I suggested how to do it. "That comment proves he's drunk," muttered JP sarcastically. But there was no need for proof – he was well away and the condition of the Great Cabin this morning proved it. Snowballing on the deck this morning. I hit Alex at short range in the ear, which gave me great satisfaction and him a splendid shock. He spluttered a lot and didn't even think (at first) that I had done it.

A magical snowstorm as we left – also, spinning dolphins (hourglass, black and white) displaying close to the bow.

22/4 – Monday - 1430

Left Stanley 0800 yesterday – most people hung over, pissed off or both. Re-starting a journey is always difficult.

Two nights out – and not seriously drunk on either.

How I hate to be in control of myself. Still, it doesn't happen often.

Where are we going next? I don't think anyone knows. The wind is in the north east. It is impossible to sail. Both engines are now running but we are only making a bare 5 knots because of the headwind. We can't possibly make Rio de Janeiro by 28th. April (published schedule) or 1st. May (revised schedule) – Chris is talking about Montevideo or somewhere instead of Rio – also, I suspect the rest of the trip, all 8,000 miles of it will now be a frantic scamper to catch ourselves up. Most of us thought the first leg schedule (over 6 knots) unattainable, the Rio date inconceivable. Why has it taken the Captain so long to come to the same conclusion?

My NewSong has turned into the story of a crew silly enough to follow their Captain anywhere:

> *The Captain said, I'll put about, I don't know where we'll go*
> *The crew all cried, Oh Captain Blake, we'll follow high or low*
> *If it's Argentine or Monte V. or Stanleyville or Stowe*
> *Just pick a chart at random and we'll sail there, quick or slow*
>
> *And the bark came round and the sails we were unfurling*
> *And we wore the ship and bore away until the day was done*
> *And it's hey for Rio Grande or it's ho for Battersea*
> *If the Captain drinks that brandy we could end in Zuyder Zee*

The next few days were dull, very dull. I hate motoring in a sailing ship and we did virtually nothing else. I read as much as I could, but even that was not much comfort:

22/4 – Monday-1930

Much as I enjoy reading rubbish, I stopped at p. 86 of a book called 'Either Way Dead' by one Tony Gyles. A very silly story about Nasty Nazis sabotaging the Queen Mary, c. 1943. Also startlingly badly written – almost every sentence starts with a participle.

One of the books I have read is a biography of Lord Cochrane by Donald Thomas, published in 1978. One passage stays with me very strongly:

> *The ship's biscuits felt "like calves' foot jelly or blancmange when swallowed because of the number of maggots in them. The (drinking) water was the colour of pear tree bark ...."*

Cochrane was the model for Jack Aubrey, the leading figure in Patrick O'Brian's books, and he was also well known to Captain Marryat, the author of Mr. Midshipman Easy, another nautical book I enjoyed re-reading. I believe Marryat served with Cochrane.

I interviewed my watchmates for Martin Morant's video about going round Cape Horn and listened to the replies with interest, Craig's especially. There always seems to be a lot going on in Craig's head.

Craig: 24/4

What do you think about when you're alone out on the bow, as the look out?

"Friends, people I'm meeting in Whitby and what I expect myself to do."

What is the biggest challenge?

"Stuff! The locker - it's the hardest thing but also the most exhilarating thing, not having any possessions."

Rounding the Horn itself:

"I was completely aware of where I was in the world - a divine experience."

Do you ever get frightened? (I meant by the sea, the storms, by climbing the rigging)

"Every day! What I'm most frightened of now is leaving the ship."

Kate, 25/4

was the only one to comment on the lack of privacy on the ship. She went on:

"I'm changing every day from this experience; it's your moulding time, your teenage years. It's so awesome (but so difficult to explain when I go home). I get all pumped about it and tell my friends about it and my friends go 'oh yeah, 63 knots of wind, is that a lot?' 'This Endeavour then is it like that ocean liner we saw?' They're never going to understand unless they come out here."

What will she say to her children about this trip? Won't they laugh at the idea of their mum climbing the rigging on a square rigger? She giggled at the question.

"They better not ..... maybe I'll send them out on some eighteenth century sailing boat, I'll say, yeah kids, it was cool."

Bernard, the French waiter from Sydney, was the only person who commented on the aesthetics of the journey, who seemed as aware as me that it was beautiful.

"The sea is different every day."

Bernard fell in love with Endeavour because he saw the picture of her in a big storm on the cover of the 2001 brochure. He decided he must sail on her at once.

Endeavour in a Storm by Katya Gerasminova-Bosky
inspired by the Endeavour brochure

For a true expression of dishevelled wildness there is nothing like a gale in the bright moonlight of a high latitude.

Joseph Conrad

It was a brave decision, for Bernard to come sailing.

I glanced into his locker while we were at sea and there were a lot of pills in it. It occurred to me immediately that a gay man of Bernard's age taking a lot of pills might have Aids or be HIV positive. It didn't seem very important. He got up the mast faster than me on more than one occasion.

Months later, staying with me in London on my narrow boat, he told me that he was HIV positive and that he had shipped on Endeavour without telling anyone about it. Once at sea, after leaving New Zealand, when there was no turning back, he told the Captain and the First Officer who were, at first, horrified.

After he explained that HIV is not a disease, that it is not transmittable except sexually or through blood, that the medication keeps it under control, they adjusted to the situation, which was never mentioned for the remainder of the voyage or to the remainder of the crew.

While finalising this, today, I emailed him to find out how he is. I am not sure I will get a reply. Bernard is not on Facebook, he doesn't seem to keep in touch with ex-Endeavour ship-mates. I hope he is still OK.

26/4 Friday

Because such a number of people had been unwell, (also because we are motoring and there was little to do on deck), Glen allowed the watches to excuse one or two persons per night from the night watch.

This produced a situation where I had a whole evening free and did not have to hurry into my hammock. It was really confusing:

> Decisions – decisions – decisions. How shall I spend my evening? It is 7pm, I have no night watch to keep. What shall I do with all this time? The first night off since 3 February! 82 or more days without an evening off.

I think all I did was relax.

27/4. Saturday

Glorious morning – bright sunshine, lots of westerly wind, all sails set but engines still turning (there is a 3 knot counter current against us and we have new crew waiting to board at Rio.) I think I must have had a (small) dose of the bug that's going round. I cannot otherwise explain the depression and self-loathing that filled my heart Tuesday/Wednesday.

I was not the only one to feel sour:

27/4. Saturday

John H. and Alex are both sick of the ship.

The boat was rolling wickedly this afternoon. It caught John H. out and he slammed right across the galley and across a table. The jars he was carrying went flying (fortunately, they were plastic, not glass). He was very tight lipped about it. He just half muttered, half shouted, the pitch rising as he spoke: "let me off this FUCKING ship!" Then he picked up the spice jars and went back to work.

We have at least fifty more days to spend at sea. They are very long days if you are unhappy.

When he first came on board, John H. was known as 'Smiling John'. That is some time ago. 'Grumpy John' and 'Scowling John' have been applied to him since. The galley assistant's job is not an easy or a happy one.

> *from Clarissa Oakes, by Patrick O'Brian:*
>
> "John Nastyface was the nickname of the galley assistant, by reason of his position."

"Can I go down below and sulk," asked Alex of Kate this afternoon. "I think I've had enough of all this water."

27/4. Saturday

Middle Watch

Glorious on deck tonight – white horses, a bright, bright moon, about 20-25 knots from the south west. It has cheered us all up. The strong adverse current has suddenly abated. On the helm, we were touching 9 knots.

"I want to go bowlin'," said Alex in the moonlight. "It's Saturday night and I want to go ten pin bowlin' – the chicks are comin' too." Alex, you're on a ship, in the middle of an ocean. "I'll wear my flanelette shirt. Bowlin'! Bowlin' an' drinkin'!" Alex! "An' fightin', right? Wear your old clothes, right? 'Cause they'll get covered in blood." Alex! "Bowlorama, rock an' bowl! We're goin' down Bowlorama tonight. Heh, Sarah, wear your miniskirt, wear your miniskirt! So that when you bend down to pick up your bowls we can look right up to heaven." Alex! "I'll shave my head and maybe get a mullet. Heh, Sarah? Have you got a flanelette T shirt?"

Another item of Ozzie vocabulary has amused me: whipper-snipper (the Australian word for a strimmer)

28/4. Sunday 0400

Layday today

Wonderful soothing night on deck – a bright, bright moon, a few stars, enough wind but an easy motion now – not like the bucketing earlier. Craig and Kate were singing that medieval roundsong about a cuckoo coming in, which was rather sweet. They did it well and affectionately and they were in tune too. When I looked over the lee side at the white, white spray of our wake, I saw my own dark silhouette on the rail of this beautiful ship, outlined by the moonshine, gliding fast along.

Good moment.

28/4. Sunday -1800

Great light, great day − thoroughly enjoyed myself (got almost nothing done). Kate now an ex-watch leader, which is a relief. I suspect she may be relieved too.

Draft e-mail- 29th. April − to send in Rio

So long since I drafted one of these − almost a month. Nearly 60 4 hour stints on deck − 120 times putting wet weather gear on and taking it off (we hope to have a tea break half way through each watch) − let us see, if it were 15 or 18 garments each time, that would make more than 1500 garments on and off in thirty days (I do not strip down to the buff each and every time). Tedious? Yes. Boring. Yes, very. Worthwhile. Yes − but only just − exhaustion and tiredness have been showing in everyone since we left the Falklands on 21st. April. It seems a year ago.

And we were all looking forward to relaxing a bit, breathing again, in Rio de Janeiro but it will not be possible. We are so far behind schedule that we will have only 36 hours (max.) in port. And we are tied so umbilically to the ship, because of gangway watches, re-provisioning and other very necessary tasks, that, as Martin put it (a little mournfully): "I think I'd rather not put in there at all. I'd rather we took on the new crew out to sea."

Well, what will be, will be. It doesn't matter. I shall survive whatever happens. A bit of me would like to get off at Rio, fly home and call the whole thing off. But I can't or won't do that. I am, however, quite short-tempered and have let Steve (who is a stupid c*** sometimes) and Kate see it. Not clever, or diplomatic or (strictly) necessary. But disliking people does help to pass the time. It almost comes to hatred. In this, as in every other bad habit I indulge on board, I doubt that I am alone.

Last week was not good at all. I think I had a mild dose of the 'flu bug we picked up in the Falklands. It made me very depressed. Since last Wednesday, I have felt much better. Also, I have broached my own books and re-read TS Eliot's Selected Poems (including the wonderful Marina) as well as the little paper back copy of Ecclesiastes which Judy gave me after I got back from the Indian Ocean. It is good to get the mind at work again, to read something challenging.

Also, just in the last twenty four hours, I have composed yet more verses of the song that I have written for John Highmore to perform at the next evening event and made four low angle astro-navigational observations which were interesting. One of them was very accurate (an intercept within a few seconds) a second much less so (within five minutes but no better). I ought to check the other two, to confirm which is definitive and whether there are real problems with the glare which (I assume) caused me not to get the best out of the horizon on one of those two. (The third that I checked was within 8 miles – not particularly good by my standards).

What I have neglected to mention, in my sour and lonely bad temper, is that the weather has improved dramatically, so that only an obstinate and pessimistic old fool like me would now bother with full wet weather gear and that yesterday was a day for many shenanigans on deck in beautiful bright sunshine, with razor cut haircuts for me, several others and (SADLY) for Jane, who had the most beautiful thick dark hair I have ever seen. I tried to disconnect the power from the clippers to protect her but was over-ruled by the mob. It was an execution, not a haircut.

"This is like murder," said one of the older crew members.

Mark you, she looks very fetching (if somewhat ambi-sexual) with her hair cut like a boy. It emphasizes her eyes, which are VERY striking.

Today is Tiffany's 25th. birthday.
Her beauty makes me sad, not because I cannot have her but because it will fade so fast.

29/4. Monday (cont.)

Bad tempered with Kate at cleaning stations. She tried to organize me again (and may have been in the right).

Infuriating!

Unfortunately, I let it show – I always do with her.

And today (30/4) she asked me to sign her tee-shirt (I wondered if she would, after my sharp words yesterday) and I wrote "bon voyage – with love."

She infuriates me as much as any daughter. And I love her just like that.

What more can one say?

30/4. Tuesday

Unexpectedly alongside in Rio Grande to visit the proposed new museum there, of nautical archaeology and history, and I have (very unexpectedly indeed) behaved sensibly. I am not joining the Gadarene rush to the pub . I am staying on board.

30/4. Tuesday - later

An hour and a half later and I am all dressed up and waiting to hit the town. I changed my mind. However, Hans has hacked his head on a low beam and Peter Bath is sewing him up (Alf did the same thing yesterday and Peter sewed him up too.)

1/5. Wednesday

Did go for a drink – did not stay for too many. Nigel did. He crawled back in at 0530 and has not been functioning at all today (again).

Journey's end concert the night before last.

22 or 23 Cape Horners due to leave the ship at Rio Grande or in Rio de Janeiro. They will be very much missed.

John H. and I rather hurriedly rendered my NewSong (which got the atmosphere going). I played the guitar, he sang (or at any rate intoned). The verse about the chippies got a good laugh - Tig's given name is Andrew and he's the Assistant to the Carpenter himself, Andy Law:

> *The Carpenter was Andy and Andy was his mate*
>
> *And while one of them was randy, well, the other one had Kate*
>
> *But both boys shared a passion which was not up for debate*
>
> *They thought slurping tea and hoarding cups was absolutely great*

John performed it really well considering we had hardly rehearsed at all. He doesn't like rehearsing. But I think it might have been rather better if we had.

My favourite verse didn't make it into the final version, for diplomatic rather than musical reasons:

> *There's one galley boss, Joanna, and the other one is Jane*
>
> *And if this song insults them, I will never eat again*
>
> *I will prob'ly die in Rio in considerable pain*
>
> *If you search the bilges for me, you will search away in vain*

Hans sang a couple of songs and recited a poem. He had made a leather Cape Horn waistcoat and got everyone to sign it on the inside. Lovely idea. I wrote: "from one stargazer to another" and signed it J., as usual. However, it looks like something from the hippy stores at Camden market. So does Hans sometimes, in his multi-coloured trousers.

Graham Santorini (the quietest man on the ship) recited Masefield's "I must go down to the sea again" from memory. He was, initially, completely inaudible. He was asked to speak up. When he started again, he roared one word in ten and swallowed three. The effect was curious but he was very brave to do it at all – a less likely poetaster I cannot imagine.

Peter Gosbell, the Second Engineer (another unlikely participant) read and recited verses by Kipling about how important it is to be able to look yourself in the face in the mirror. (The first line is "when you get what you want in this struggle for self")

It is not a poem I know but he did it very well.

One night watch, Pete told me how his relationship with his ex. had come apart.

"It was all right for the first five years," he said, "then it was all 'come back to Adelaide,' we got to get married in fucking Adelaide because of her dad, fucking Bulgarian, you know, fucking thought he was in fucking old Bulgaria like she had to fucking do what he said. All the fucking time."

"You're well out of it," I said.

"That's what me fucking father said. She gave me the fucking ring back."

Pete is 33 years old – the girl was about to turn 30. They had been together for seven years. That probably says it all.

She also wanted him to give up marine engineering, as well as settle down – she would not have married him if he went on travelling.

"When she heard I was going round the Horn, well, I thought she'd be fucking pleased like. She just said, 'you're still chasing dreams, Pete, you're just running away.'

As the ship eventually docked at Rio de Janeiro, a small airliner prepared to take off from a runway very close to the water. Pete watched it with something like greed in his eyes.

"Christ, I love fucking engineering," he said.

The engineers round Cape Horn were called Alf and Pete.

Alf never let a swear word cross his lips but Pete made up for it.

Pete was in foremast watch with me and he joined in a lot considering he had all his other duties in the Engine Room.

The lavatories on board often required attention and, needless to say, I took the piss out of the two of them in my NewSong.

> Our good ship had two engineers, both full of beans and fit
> They liked playing with their spanners and dabbling in the ****
> And they fixed the heads a dozen times without an angry word
> But each morning, floating in the bowl, you'd find another ****

I tried to spread the sarcasm around as evenly as I could.

"Who's next?" asked John threateningly as he geared up to sight read another verse.

It was, of course, Glen, the First Officer:

> The First Mate had a wardrobe that would make a peacock blush
> And he said, oh Captain, Captain, must we berth in such a rush
> There are items of apparel that I haven't even worn
> And the buttons on my waistcoat won't be finished till the dawn ....

Glen made us perform my NewSong at the beginning of the evening and it helped to get the atmosphere going. But it would, I thought, have been better towards the end, as the climax of the proceedings.

I felt my nice shiny NewSong was wasted a bit - pearls before swine?

Since last night, Hans, Lauren and Joe have all said how good it was. But that, of course, is not enough. I would now like to know what the other 53 people on board thought.

Footnote - 6/5

I have now inveigled JP and the Captain into saying how good the song was. I am waiting for a chance to corner Ruth and Martin as well.

Footnote2 - 17/5

I finally managed to mention the song to Martin, who couldn't remember it at all!

Collapse of stout party .... I deserved that.

*****

The author at Cape Horn

Rio Grande was an unscheduled stop a few hundred miles south of Rio de Janeiro to put everyone ashore who was in a desperate hurry. I asked one of them to email a message on my behalf:

ben.gilbert@ebone.com
cc headcreative@unforgettable.com
30/4/02 afloat near Rio Grande.

Hi, to you both – please send this on to the gang, esp. to Mark Eisenthal. It is a very hurried e-mail which will be forwarded to you, with luck, by one of my shipmates .....

We are well and will be in Rio de Janeiro in about five days – however, we are behind schedule and I may not get time to contact you from there.

Rounding the Horn was fantastic! Calm and beautiful, in the early morning, with a beautiful sunrise, after weeks of dull passage work, several serious storms and many black cold nights on watch with no stars to be seen. The boat is beautiful and so strong that you cannot believe it. "No sea can harm her," wrote Captain Cook about the original Endeavour and I think he may have been right.

The hardships are bearable (apart from the boredom which is terrific). The thought of sleeping in a bed and eating and living normally is quite disconcerting. In some ways I shall be relieved not to get off the boat in Rio – it is easier to stay rooted in the routines than to re-invent them.

I am in super health and we are all starting to enjoy the much warmer weather. It was horribly cold on deck for most of the last two months. I have had the sort of brutally short haircut which soldiers get when they join up for the Army and everyone says that it suits me. It was certainly much cheaper than my usual haircut ... Did anyone get the postcards from the Falkland Islands yet? More postcards from Rio, come what may ...

So – if I do not make electronic contact from Rio, you will know why. In the Azores, around 23 May, is the next best chance.

3/5 Friday

Rolling painfully, still under power.

I fell heavily on the foredeck last night (as did Bernard). I trod on a rope which shouldn't have been there and it just rolled over underfoot, me with it. The deck is filled with ropes, lines, sails, all the clutter associated with rigging work. There is tar everywhere you walk, on everything you touch. The moon rose late last night and the sky was black and the ship was very dark and treacherous. My wrist, on which I fell, is very sore. I thought for one moment that I had broken it.

Since the Falklands, 21/4, I think we have sailed 3 days (27, 28, 29 April).

Motoring is horrible in a sailing boat. I hated it when I was with Dan in the Red Sea and I hate it even more on board Endeavour.

It is not what sailing boats are for.

5/5 Sunday - 1445

Approaching Rio de Janeiro on a glassily calm sea still under power. There is a refreshing breeze on deck but everywhere below is tropical (the extractor fans have failed in the galley). Stood Middle Watch this morning under a beautiful sky and the dawn was pretty though not spectacular. Cold on deck, in the dark. Everyone mocks the shopping bag in which I carry all my spare gear around, especially Jennaya who has christened it the Granny bag but it comes in awfully useful when there is a sudden rainstorm or I need extra garments.

One of the exhaust fans has failed as well − we had a fire alarm go off at 1710 or 1715 yesterday, just as we were about to gather on the quarterdeck for a sundowner.

Incidentally, there was a distinct green flash at sunset last night, covering only the tiny fragment of the sun's disk remaining above the horizon at the critical moment. There was no radiant or halo effect.

I have never seen a green flash before, it is quite rare. Some people claim it is mythical. We all saw it, for an instant.

6/5 Monday

Names of those leaving the ship at Rio Grande and Rio de Janeiro

Dr. Peter Bath, Bob the Jailer (he looked after one of the Kray brothers), John Ellis, quiet Alex (not to be confused with rather loud Alex, the one in foremast watch), Peter Thomas one of the supernumeraries, David McGovern from BT, Rossi from Boston, Bernard the French waiter, Joe the mud doctor, Michael the other supernumerary, Malcolm Evans with his Powerbook and his Canon Digital camera, Peter Gosbell the superfit fucking engineer, the beautiful, beautiful G.I. Jane (now with very short hair) and Steve Winnick.

Good companions, all. I miss them.

What a range of people you meet, when you go sailing.

6/5/2002
to my youngest son, Josh

We got to Rio last night - we hope to leave again early tomorrow. It is all a bit of a panic because we are trying to catch up with our schedule by shortening the shore stops.

Anyway, all is well, I am having a great time and you will (I hope) be receiving a news-type circular sent to Ben and Judy. Just in case that does not reach you, here is the briefest possible version of my news.

I am determined to spend this afternoon, my one afternoon in Rio (a place I have never visited) on the beach at Copacabana and not in an internet cafe.

Endeavour still entirely magical - the most wonderful ship to sail. And the monotony and relative hardship (cold!) of the passage has been tolerable - you can get used to just about anything if you have to. Biggest storm so far featured 63 knots of apparent wind but going round the Horn was spectacular and unexpected - calm, almost glassy seas, just enough wind to move us along, dawn breaking over the Horn itself (and we were very close to it), a sip of sparkling wine, some speeches, songs, tears, cheers, celebrations and a million snapshots. The next day another big storm hit us in the middle of the night and we flew up to the Falkland Islands in 45-50 knots of wind from the south west where it snowed like mad which the young Australians thought pretty special - most of them have never seen snow or sleet before.

Worst moments? There was one night, in 45-50 knots, in the dark, with the boat being thrown around like a child's toy when I did not think I could physically manage to get out onto the main course yard to furl the sail. And, when I managed to get on, it was all I could do to hold on and to safeguard myself. But we got the sail furled, in the end. It just took rather a long and nail-biting amount of time. Dougal, the boatswain, said it was the most difficult furl he had ever been involved with. Who am I to argue?

Best moments? When you think you have done everything you can. When you get to sleep. When you can lie in, on a Sunday (lay day). When you are warm enough on watch. When you write a song about what goes on on this vessel and people laugh at it and enjoy it, perhaps even remember it. There have been some very good moments.It's been very special. I wouldn't have missed it. It's one of the great journeys and to complete it in a square rigger is an achievment that will mean a lot to me. Nothing really compares (except sailing with Dan on Domain).

See you all soon. I do miss you - lots.

All the best, and lots of love, J.

*****

7/5/02
to Judy Head, my former lover and good friend

How am I? Bloody sore, that's how - walking the city streets yesterday has taken its toll on my knees and my muscles - I always forget how quickly they atrophy on board ship.

Rio doesn't seem very special compared to the other great cities, New York, Rome, Milan, Paris, Sydney and Perth - however, a pleasant meal with two large strong beers last night cost less than $8 (US) which cannot be bad - my only extravagance so far has been sending postcards - v. expensive indeed, by local standards.

It was absolutely great to hear from you this morning - the girls are gorgeous here and I have sent you a fairly filthy postcard from Copacabana. Brazilian magazines, I have noticed, include the widely distributed 'Positacoes Amorasas' (love-making positions) which is advertised on every news stand with only the practical bits blanked out - also, a magazine called 'Plastic'which features suspiciously buxom blondes. Travel does broaden the mind, doesn't it? I woke up in my hammock this morning dreaming of wenches (what else) with an embarrassingly large erection and nowhere to put it ..... I have definitely been at sea too long.

I have been managing to scribble regularly and (bliss) a friend on board called Martin lets me use his personal computer to type up the notes; in return, I am making a video about Martin's exploits on board for his grandson. He is on board with his wife, Ruth - small, determined, of a similar age. He is 72 and still climbs the rigging and helps to furl the sails. She doesn't climb but joins in otherwise with enthusiasm.

Endeavour is the sexiest vessel ever - only Domain compares (and you know how I felt about Domain). The routine is hard, boring and often very irritating but I am having a lovely time, as usual, except when we have to use the engines because there is no wind. We have had no wind since the Falklands (about 10 days ago) but the day before we got to the Falklands we set the all time 24 hours record for Endeavour under sail - 202 miles (Domain's best ever was about 185). After that, we got stuck in a high pressure area and nothing much moved for days. So we motored. And motored. And motored. I do hate motoring. But we need to. This is an eighteenth century ship on a 21st. century schedule. That's not an ideal arrangement.

This ship (like all ships) seethes with misinformation about almost everything, especially arrival dates. But I will be very impressed and surprised if we make it to Whitby on 21st. June, as originally scheduled. On the other hand, Endeavour usually does achieve the dates forecast for the end of a journey, however late she runs at intermediate stops.

Incidentally, my respect for Chris Blake (and even a certain grudging affection) has come along a lot. The last song I wrote on board made much of the recent indecision about where to go and also touched on his habits when on shore. The refrain climaxed in the lines: "So it's hey for Rio Grande and it's ho for Battersea, and if the Captain drinks that brandy we could end in Zuyder Zee." It went down quite well.

Listen, my dear, I must stop writing. It is quite expensive to compose online here and I have three other new e-mails to scrutinise. I will be in touch asap.

Postcards of girls, virtually naked, on Copacabana Beach to Dan, Judy, Sue L., Ben and the other boys:

"So it takes 59 years and 10,000 miles on a square rigger to get me to Copacabana Beach and what's happening when I get there? It's raining, that's what. Not a thong in sight. Even the muggers have taken shelter. But it was the moodiest beachscape I ever saw."

It was supposed to be a flying visit to Rio. But there were local complications, with the agents and with payments.

I never knew the full story. I never quite understood the problem, though I had my suspicions. So we were stuck there for almost a week, moored in the financial district beside a museum and the problem was that we had to report back to the ship every four hours, in case the complications had suddenly dissolved and our stores and fuel were ready to come on board and we might suddenly be ready to depart. We wandered about the city rather aimlessly and very foot-sore. It was a long time since we had pounded pavements.

And the ship, tied up and lifeless, was not much of a haven - the Captain was worried, the First Officer was impatient; those of us who were going on to England were anxious to get back to sea and many of those who had left the ship were hanging around rather desperately to wave farewell to Endeavour when she eventually departed. It was not a happy time.

Ruth and Martin, always so stalwart, thought for a moment of leaving the ship and taking a break and flying to the Azores to re-join. I didn't want to do that. The moment of despair had passed in New Zealand and I was tired but not disquieted about continuing. Life is sometimes about enduring, being able to endure, and so - quite often - is sailing.

But I had a lot of time to write emails:

8/5/02
to Sharon, from the BBC gang

Hello my darling! I am stuck in Rio because we have no food/fuel for the ship. Everything is very manana round here so heaven knows when we will get going. Anyway, it has given me a chance to tidy and check my emails and I will send you a postcard later on.
Last night was a farewell dinner and I was extremely well behaved and abstemious until about midnight. Then we went out for a last drink. Come three in the morning, severely poorer, I was trying desperately to climb into my hot sweaty hammock and the wake up call at 0715 is still ringing in my ears three hours later. "Don't crunch your toast so loud," I muttered at breakfast. "Must you slurp your coffee so noisily?" came the reply. I think an early beer may be the answer - that, at least, I can look forward to.
Lots of love from a very fragile navigator (retired)

Sharon e-mailed me back that she is divorced now, has had a a few unsuccessful liaisons in the last few months and is looking for a thirty something. I mail back that I'm a thirty something, there's just rather a lot of the something. I await her response with interest. I always fancied Sharon.

Rio has always been reputed to be a dangerous city so I tried to keep my wits about me even when alcohol intervened.

7/5 Tuesday

In the afternoon, the sound of a shot on the Avenue Presidente Vargas – a few interested parties turn towards the noise but no surprise or much excitement. A portly (hatless) gentleman in uniform running, in the crowded central reservation of the eight lane boulevard which is stiff with traffic. He has his gun out but I don't see him fire it. Within a few seconds the interest dies away. There are no more shots. The day goes on.

20 minutes later, further south on the same Avenue, two street boys sprint through the crowd, sidestepping and dodging like eels. Neither of them seemed to be carrying anything but two indignant sweaty men are in reluctant pursuit. The crowd closes in around the incident and I learn no more about it.

Dangerous? Perhaps - but probably no worse than many other cities. Alex went to sleep on a bus and woke unscathed. Kevin did the same in the post office. I did not care to go to sit in a park in daylight in the city centre - because you can be very vulnerable in parks - but Nigel went to sleep in the gutter outside a bank. "No, it was not in the gutter," he said indignantly. He claimed he was definitely in the porch of the bank, at least eight foot from the gutter.

John Ellis and Peter Bath were reputed to have been robbed of their dollars at gun or knife point on Copacabana Beach. But this turned out to be a complete fabrication, a sort of Chinese whispers story, perhaps starting with the German film crew who joined us at Rio, who might have misunderstood something.

Malcolm, the guy with the digital camera, lost all his personal possessions and lots of dollars when he got out of a taxi and it took off unexpectedly with all his gear. The poor bastard lost all the cash given to him for the CD of his Endeavour pictures which he intends to turn out and which lots of the crew had pre-ordered and pre-paid.

The taxi driver returned the lot.

A local is reputed to have accompanied some of the gang to Copacabana Beach. But he would not accompany them across the sand to the water. "Too dangerous," he said, shaking his head.

I think I felt less at risk in Rio than sometimes in London – the same rules applied – do not carry things that look valuable, walk fast and with purpose, do not stand on strange street corners looking lost or like a stranger to the city.

Out looking for a restaurant one evening with Martin, Ruth and Jeanine (who joined the ship in Rio but knew Endeavour and Ruth and Martin before), I got worried. We were conspicuously foreign, speaking loudly in English, not knowing where we were going. The streets in the financial district were dark and empty. I felt we were a potential target and was glad when we retreated to Ruth and Martin's hotel and got ourselves off the streets.

It turned out to be a very civilized and pleasant evening, a buffet in the upstairs restaurant of their hotel, with two bottles of good Chilean wine (Concha y Toro Cabernet Sauvignon) and some civilized conversation.

As Jeanine and I walked back to the ship after the meal, a young man was energetically fucking his wench on the central reservation under the fly over. I thought he might take time out to come and mug us but he plunged on – he had other and much more interesting priorities.

I would certainly have felt the same.

8/5 to Mark

Ship still stuck in Rio - our agent seems unable to organize food and fuel for us .... I have sore feet from walking city streets for the first time in three months and have spent all the money I wanted to spend, largely on beer, nice food, postcards and the internet. Brazilian wine not too good but the girls are gorgeous and Rio has a surprisingly un-frenetic and gentle atmosphere, given its doubtful reputation. I think I could happily live here.

8/5 Wednesday

No deliveries to the ship, no progress, we are stuck here at least until this afternoon. Michael the supernumerary very generously stood us all dinner last night and, with extra beer taken afterwards in the company of Kevin, John H. and Tony, I am a touch fragile. I think I will go and buy myself a new notebook, which will comfort me and then settle somewhere to write about the people on board the ship. I wrote a little while ago that the young people were pairing off. The latest gossip is that JP and Clare are an item, also Pete Gos. and Jo, Simon and Jane and perhaps Andy and Sarah − I think the last two are just good mates, but they certainly enjoy each other's company.

Uncertain what to do with myself today. It is too dangerous to go to the beach by myself and my feet and legs are too sore for me to walk. I will have a large beer very soon, which should start to restore me.

8/5 - in a pavement cafe

New notebooks make me feel clean and organized − but there, I have made a mistake already. I have blotted my copybook. Small notebooks make me write more urgently and sometimes smaller − to fit it all in.

Setting an old notebook aside generates an odd sense of loss. Surely there was unfinished business in those damp, blurred, mangled, crowded pages? Notes to be added, references to be checked, lists to be completed? Well, it is all over now. Checked or not.

8/5 - in another pavement café

Third world city? Not by comparison with others I have seen. The Metro is cleaner than the underground in London. The traffic circulates fast, without much fuss or stress (no horns). An old man sprawled unconscious in a doorway. His hat had fallen off. He might have been dead. Within 5 minutes - I happened to be watching - three or four people stopped and looked closely at him. One girl bent down and delicately checked his pulse. Would Londoners have done that? Three or four of them? I doubt.

Rio is a large, sprawling city. I have only seen a tiny bit of it. I am told the shanty towns on the outskirts (favelas) are horrific. But it still stands up well to comparisons with Cairo, Moscow – and London.

No flies either.

The temperature is 26 degrees C – day and night – muggy rains in the afternoon, refreshing breeze most of the time.

I went to visit the first Festival de Humor Grafico (cartoons) displayed, for some unfathomable reason, at the Palace of Justice.

Da Costa Junior (one of the artists) draws men who are all eyes and noses – he shows a one man spacecraft, an infinity of stars behind it – but the cute little pilot has hanged himself and dangles from the spaceship's door – a horribly sad (and beautiful) image. Most of his pictures are more funny than this, and a bit less disturbing.

9/5 – 0828 – on the quayside by the nautical museum

Another day hanging fire in Rio – oh dear! Whoever it is that we have failed to bribe is definitely angry. Four full days in port and no food has been delivered, no fuel made available. We are, of course, starting to run short of water – we cannot use the watermaker in port. Last I heard we had only 6,000 litres (6 tonnes) – enough for 2-3 days. The danger is that tomorrow is Friday and that we may get stuck till Monday or Tuesday.

I had a lot of time to spend in cafes and restaurants in Rio. I liked the place - a lot. The street kids are all over the place, begging, stealing, trying to survive (the fundamental human imperative - that and breeding). I made a very terse note in my diary, to remind myself:

Street kids and the unexpected tolerance with which the waiters react to them. It's as if they are thinking 'there but for the Grace of God, go I.'

This, surely, is the Rainbow Nation.

10/5 – still stuck in Rio – FRIDAY! oh dear!

So much for the quick stop in Rio to catch up with the schedule. We are still here, five days later, still without fuel, food or clearance to leave. Oh dear! Oh dear! There have been negotiations and protests and heaven knows what. We are front page news in Brazil's national newspapers and on television, but it is not doing us any good at all.

Sadly, we have not been able to use the time to see more of Rio or Brazil. We keep having to report back to the ship to find out what is going on (nothing!)

Last night a fuel barge was due alongside at 1800 - it turned up at 2300, without the right fittings for the job. It was due back at 0900 but this is now after 1100 and there is no sign of it. All very frustrating.

My own theory is that we have offended someone very important (there was a change of local agent at the last minute) and everything to do with us has been put at the bottom of the pile .... no doubt we will get out of here eventually but it is all a bit grim, for the old lags like me and almost worse for the new people, who are joining the ship as well. We are also running out of ship's water and have no obvious source of alternative supply .... as for the sewage arrangements, I will draw a veil.

10/5 - Friday

It gets worse. Chris Blake has appealed to all of us to lend the Endeavour 29,000 reals – about 12,000 dollars (U.S) to pay the agent and let us get away. (This amount is in addition to the cost of fuel and food, which has already been paid). Lots of us have been trooping to the ATMs this afternoon and will be trooping out for a second bite at the cherry tomorrow. I went as bodyguard with Ruth and Martin to get money from their bank accounts but three out of my four credit cards are not working here - I didn't advance any of my own money because I couldn't access it.

Anyway, I am not sure I think this is a good idea:

1) I doubt if enough money can be raised and wonder who will defray interest costs and charges incurred.
2) Will it work? the agent, banks and authorities seem all to have it in for us – why should money resolve that? (especially over a weekend)

"I am so pissed off with this place," muttered Tony indistinctly last night.

But I loved Rio, except for the circumstances. Brazil is intoxicating, the rhythm, the noise, the vitality, the danger, the beauty. Like nowhere else I've been. I might have to come back – it's that bad. No smartness here, no style fetish like in Milan and Rome, just huge confidence, energy and vitality.

We went for drinks to the Rua do Commercio. Steve and Joe (who have left the boat) were there – also Tony and Kevin. The noise was shattering, the crowd pressed shoulder to shoulder, bopping systematically, enthusiastically and with commitment (as Brazilians do) to the fierce rhythms of a live band on the corner of the street, which is more of a narrow alley, overhung by tall tenement blocks whose inhabitants get a grandstand view of the performances as well as fiercely amplified sound at more than 100 decibels. This band had no platform (it is not there to be looked at but to be heard) and only the singer (more a chanter) seemed to have a microphone. But the crowd all knew his songs and the choruses of his songs and they surrounded him and his band with a lovely possessiveness and a vast warm pressure of enthusiasm. It was <u>their</u> music. This was the line up: two players on little four stringed mini guitars (I think they are called cavaquinhos) – who thrummed away like mad – about four drummers including the dominant male on the big bass drum and the singer himself. It was wonderfully convincing. I loved it. I really relished it. We were sitting down, listening, watching (you couldn't talk) drinking a few beers and then I wanted to leave and started to shuffle forward with the crowd swaying and bopping around me, pressing on me (and my hand very firmly on my wallet in my right hand trouser pocket - just in case).

I walked round the corner and then back towards the ship and stopped for a final beer and met a Civil Service systems analyst covered in shit in the bar at the corner of Rua do Rosario. He stank rather, as his friend kept pointing out to him (the friend poured a glass of water over his trousers). His name was Adelberto. and he had inadvertently waded through something noxious, that was very evident - but I never learned why or what. His English was adequate but not for that.

It was easy to leave the pubs in Bluff, in New Zealand, or in the Falklands. They were not much fun.

To leave the cafés in Rio?

Impossible!

One night, I ended up playing the guitar in one, swapping riffs with an amazing oldish male/singer player – grey hair, huge protruding eyes – in the café just round the corner from the boat. Unforgettable. I couldn't leave.

Only I wish I had danced while I was there.

"Chopp" (draft beer) and "obligado" (thank you). The only Brazilian Portugese words I have mastered.

Leaving the coast behind

The fourth leg

Rio de Janeiro to the Azores via Cape Verde Islands - 3,974 miles

11/5 - Saturday

"The best possible view of Rio," said Ruth Morant as we left it. The cash the crew raised was enough - it worked!

The t'gallant masts are aloft again - when did we do that? I think I must have been ashore.

11/5 – Saturday - 1530

We are heading up the coast, close in, with a favourable current of something more than one knot. Four watch system now, instead of the three watch system we have been used to. I am in Starboard B, most of former foremast in Starboard A. I am away from both Alex and Kate (a good thing) but Jennaya and Ally are the watchleaders. They are very childish together, which irritates the hell out of me.

12/5 - Sunday

Because I am in a different watch, I have had to move my hammock, which is another irritant. In fact I was distinctly crabby yesterday but today is so beautiful, bright, clear and calm with virtually no wind and a pretty line of fluffy clouds at the horizon, that only a fool could not enjoy being out here.

13/5 – Monday - 0729

Another glorious morning (with virtually no wind). We have been on since 0400 and I am scribbling this while on stern watch.

We are about five miles off the coast, hugging the shore to find the counter current. It is over 90 F down below.

14/5 - Tuesday

Still motoring. Honestly, if this journey came to an end tomorrow, it would not be too soon.

Will I enjoy any of the rest of it now? I just feel thoroughly jaded, almost angry with it all. I am not alone.

Nigel discussed getting off in Rio with his wife over the telephone.

Martin and Ruth never got the shuttle to see their friend in Sao Paolo – but the idea of an airport, with a possible flight to the Azores or even straight back to Heathrow, definitely flitted through their minds.

Pete the Fish said (interestingly) that I "seemed much more happy" since the split watch system removed me from suffering the company of Alex, Kate and Craig for more than ten hours each day. I am surprised that it shows. I always think I can conceal my feelings more efficiently than I do

But I certainly feel that 900 hours together has been enough. I adore many of Alex's various personalities but he does have rather a lot of them, several very strident.

15/5 Wed.

Woke at 0530, but not too tired. Heading 040, wind 30 on the starboard bow – making progress but with no help from the elements.

Afternoon maintenance, which I hate, I set myself to repaint the rough tree rail and do a really proper job – instead, I spilled a large quantity of white paint on the precious and beautifully scoured deck.

Mortifying!

Andy and the others very cool about it – not me.

Was I happier today because I tried harder? Because no one hassled me? Because of the sinister chemistry of the brain? I wish I knew.

But I was happier. In spite of the accident. It took me four days to scrape all the paint off the deck.

16/5 - Thursday - 1100

Sailing, very slowly. It is suddenly quiet and wet (it is raining and overcast - essentially calm). We will not be able to continue to sail on this course unless the wind veers 2 or more points (around 23 degrees) so it is only temporary but a blessing all the same - it is nearly a month since we sailed.

17/5 - Friday

Another day when I feel mysteriously content - as if I could be happy anywhere, under any conditions. Dawn was beautiful. Motoring again (and the port engine playing up) . What wind there is from the east and our course is 065M - roughly north east

Much later: 2015.

About to go to bed: no change in wind, or mood.

Everyone talked to me today. Chris Penfold (70) about almost every sailing trip he ever took, Jeanine about her last movie, Alf about putting one of his sons through college, Ally about the subject of a sea shanty (which he then sang to me). Even the Captain stopped and chatted though the conversation faded away unnervingly after one or two exchanges, as it always does with him.

Ben also talked me, at some length, about how the BBC voyage in 2001 had just been "an ordinary voyage with rotten food" and it was supposed to be so much more than that, he said. He had expected it to be a cross between an endurance test and an exercise in practical archaeology, genuinely re-creating the living conditions on an eighteenth century ship.

So it is clear that the Endeavour's professional crew expected the BBC trip to be quite, quite different, much more exacting, much more testing.

No wonder they were disappointed - with the participants (us) and with what went on.

18/5 - Saturday

Captain's Rounds. Only 4 to go. Still under engine. Brazilian coast receding.

"Wine tasting" last night. Reg gave a rather basic talk about wine and then people got surprisingly drunk. Jane took Simon in the breast hooks, which put him in a very good mood. Then Penguin bunked off with Ben and was 16 minutes late for the watch, which put Simon in a very bad mood. Jane was also spotted leaving the pinnace with Craig. What interesting lives they all do lead!

19/5 - Sunday

Sailing again at last, t'gallants set, sprits'l drawing, sprit tops'ls ready to bend on. Thank goodness for that. It is a great relief.

20/5 - Monday

My eldest son, Ben, is 35 today. I gave Tony a biscuit to celebrate.

20/5 - Monday (cont.)

Very very little wild life since Stanley. A few petrels and rails - boobies, of course and dolphins at night (it is said) - I haven't seen any myself. Flying fish plentiful - but the deck of Endeavour is too high for them to come on board which is a shame. I've always wanted to eat one for breakfast.

Beautiful calm conditions - beautifully accurate sights. No wind at all. Heart breaking!

21/5 - Tuesday

Under engine - it is a month since we left Stanley. Between Stanley and Rio we sailed only 3 days (in about 16). Between Rio and here we have sailed only 1 (in 10). Awful!

Tiredness - I wrote so much about my tiredness between Fremantle and Hobart that I was embarrassed. I am still tired all the time. I could sleep anywhere (and did between 1300 and 1415 on a mattress in the Marines, still with my glasses on my nose). Gary once said he had gone to sleep next to a man using a needle gun (which is an astonishingly noisy piece of kit). I believe him. I think I could do the same.

There is a lot of whispering in corners at the moment. We are crossing the Equator later today and anyone who has not crossed it before is in for it.

King's Neptune's Court has been convened tomorrow, with Dougal the boatswain in charge and Gerald lending it authority and all sorts of nasty things are being planned.

Glen, the First Officer, has never crossed the line before. Nor has Andy, the shipwright - nor has Nigel Longster, who could be very obstreperous indeed if he wanted to be and seems to be planning just that.

I crossed the line for the first time in the Indian Ocean and King Neptune (in the shape of my solitary shipmate) woke me up when I was not on watch and materialised in the darkness with a trident, a crown and a bowl of something ghastly with which to anoint me. It might have been porridge. I never dared to ask. It was very theatrical. I think he recited in Latin.

But, as a result, I am part of King Neptune's Court and will not be a victim. I am to play Aphrodite, King Neptune's wife, the first time in my life I have ever dragged up.

That will be interesting ..... I am looking forward to it.

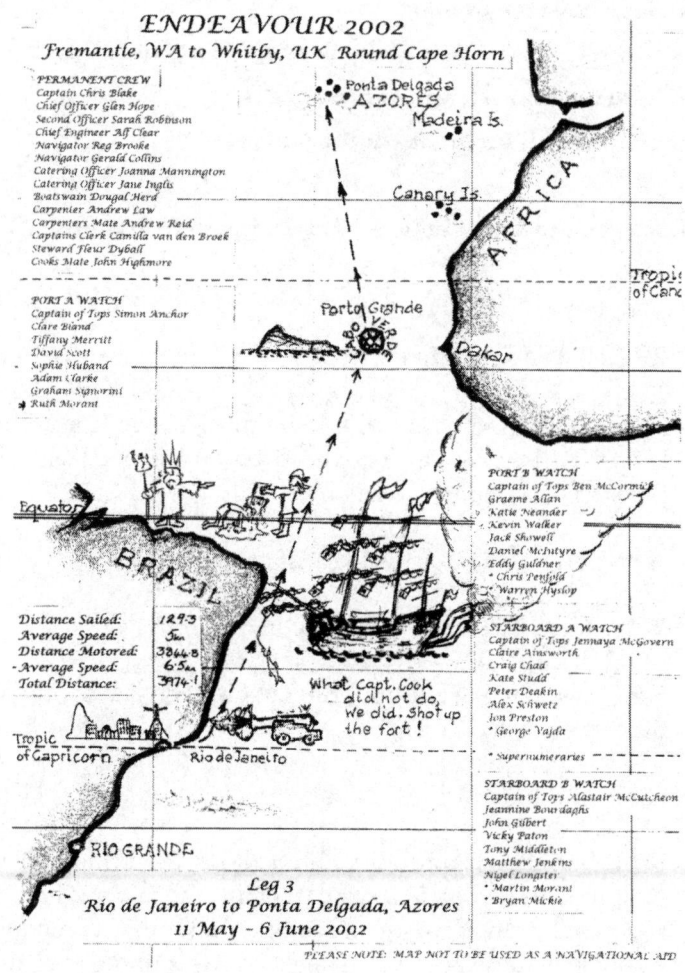

ENDEAVOUR 2002
Fremantle, WA to Whitby, UK Round Cape Horn

PERMANENT CREW
Captain Chris Blake
Chief Officer Glen Hope
Second Officer Sarah Robinson
Chief Engineer Alf Clear
Navigator Reg Brooke
Navigator Gerald Collins
Catering Officer Joanna Mannington
Catering Officer Jane Inglis
Boatswain Dougal Herd
Carpenter Andrew Law
Carpenters Mate Andrew Reid
Captains Clerk Camilla van den Broek
Steward Fleur Dyball
Cooks Mate John Highmore

PORT A WATCH
Captain of Tops Simon Anchor
Clare Bland
Tiffany Merritt
David Scott
Sophie Huband
Adam Clarke
Graham Signorini
Ruth Morant

PORT B WATCH
Captain of Tops Ben McCormick
Graeme Allan
Katie Neander
Kevin Walker
Jack Showell
Daniel McIntyre
Eddy Guldner
Chris Penfold
Warren Hyslop

STARBOARD A WATCH
Captain of Tops Jennaya McGovern
Claire Ainsworth
Craig Chad
Kate Studd
Peter Deakin
Alex Schwetz
Ian Preston
George Vajda

* Supernumeraries

STARBOARD B WATCH
Captain of Tops Alastair McCutcheon
Jeannine Bou daghs
John Gilbert
Vicky Paton
Tony Middleton
Matthew Jenkins
Nigel Longster
Martin Morant
Bryan Mickie

Distance Sailed: 1293
Average Speed: 5 kn
Distance Motored: 3846.8
Average Speed: 6.5 kn
Total Distance: 3974.1

What Capt. Cook did not do, we did. Shot up the fort!

Equator

BRAZIL

Tropic of Cancer

Tropic of Capricorn   Rio de Janeiro

Ponta Delgada
AZORES
Madeira Is.
Canary Is.
AFRICA
Porto Grande
Dakar
CAPE VERDE

RIO GRANDE

Leg 3
Rio de Janeiro to Ponta Delgada, Azores
11 May – 6 June 2002

PLEASE NOTE: MAP NOT TO BE USED AS A NAVIGATIONAL AID

CROSSING THE LINE

Gerald, one of the navigators, a big man with a resonant Irish voice, wrote a splendid speech for King Neptune and delivered it with gusto over the ship's tannoy:

I, NEPTUNE REX,

Emperor of the Deep, King of Kings, Exalted Above All Others.

He who pays homage to none.

He who commands the fish of the seas to do his bidding.

He who instructs the nymphs of the oceans.

He who controls all life beneath the waves.

Commands you to kneel before Him and pay his tribute .....

22/5 - Wednesday

Neptune ceremony at 1400 - a bit nastier than it need have been? Tarpaulins all over the deck and a huge barrel of filthy stuff to anoint the newbies.

'Top slop' said Dougal with satisfaction.

Was there really used engine oil in it?

Kate was quite vicious to those crossing the line for the first time (they included Tig).

Glen (and Jane Inglis) got it big.

I dragged up as Aphrodite and it didn't do a thing for me. First time in my life in a woman's costume and yet I did not feel, walk, think or speak any differently. I remained stubbornly myself though Craig said I was unrecognizable.

I found that rather disappointing. I have seen all sorts of men drag up over the years, in theatres, tv studios, on Endeavour on Valentine's day.

It clearly turned some of them on. They got quite excited about it.

Why not me?

Camilla, the Captain's Clerk, wrote this account of crossing the line:

Two by two, we were summoned by King Neptune.

Ruth and Martin Morant dressed in ghoulish costumes blindfolded the victims and led them to the waist of the ship amid screams and cackles from the Court. When the blindfolds were removed we were confronted with a most hideous sight - the green dread-locked Neptune Rex, the Hideous Surgeon, the Vile Executioner and the Loathsome Barber plus a whole assortment of very gruesome characters. The worst part was the stench coming from a large barrel filled with the most putrid ingredients imaginable.

Confronted by a sight beyond our worst nightmares, we were made to kneel before Neptune and his Court and plead our case. Begging had no effect and only seemed to incur more of the Court's wrath, as Glen, Chief Officer, found out when reading out his well-written plea for clemency. Tallow was rubbed into hair by the barber, stinking handfuls of rotting bin refuse was stuffed down our shirts and shorts, sauerkraut and flour was thrown over us while the Executioner tried to saw off our limbs. Once we'd endured this initiation ceremony we were 'One of Them' and were hosed and washed down with the fire hose.

It took an awful lot of scrubbing to rid our bodies of the foul stench. But we had 'Crossed the Line' and survived!

*****

NAVIGATION

Let's think about Harrison the Chronometer and Nevil Maskelyne and Dava Sobel.

Sobel's hugely successful book "Longitude" was wonderful in that it introduced the history of the Longitude problem to a wide audience and made Harrison famous. It was not, however, very fair to Nevil Maskelyne and to the lunar distance method of navigation which he pioneered.

Lunar distance measurements are simple to explain and very difficult to employ.

Briefly, if a mariner can use a sextant to measure the angular distance between the moon and the sun or a known star or planet, he can work out the time of day at his home base - Greenwich, Paris or Rome.

If he knows the time at home and compares it with local time in the South Seas or wherever he finds himself, he can work out his approximate longitude, that is how far he has come round the world since he left home. The difference in time tells him his approximate position.

A chronometer carries 'home time' accurately onto a ship and preserves it. We know that, we take it for granted. We all have electronic chronometers on our wrists or built into our mobile phones.

But it was a small miracle that any mechanical clock could accurately carry time overseas for a long period, when exposed to salt water, widely varying temperatures and the ministrations of seamen who are not always delicate with machinery of any sort.

Put yourself in Nevill Maskelyne's position, in the eighteenth century.

Clocks at that time meant pendulum clocks - completely unviable at sea. The possibility that a carpenter could invent a gadget which would function accurately at differing temperatures when bucketing around in an ocean-going ship was virtually inconceivable. No sensible person would have suggested it.

Harrison was not, in those terms, sensible. He made a clock out of lignum vitae. He was a carpenter and a genius and he created what generations of seamen called the chronometer, a spring-powered clock, with a double escapement mechanism to control the spring and the appropriate mixture of metals to control temperature variations.

What an achievment! What a magical thing to have done.

And, of course, Nevil Maskelyne was quite right to be sceptical, he was right to assume that Harrison was mistaken and was working on the wrong lines.

Carpenters? Chronometers? Bah! Humbug! Not a chance!

Captain Cook was a pragmatic man. Within ten years of the chronometer's first proving voyages, he was using a copy in anger, relying on it, testing it, adopting that very practical (and scientific) approach which I believe was utterly characteristic of men who went all over the world in wooden vessels held together and powered by miles of hemp rope and sturdy canvas.

But how did he check his chronometer?

By calculating lunar distance measurements, of course.

For more than a century, from Cook's time until about 1906, it was axiomatic that a diligent navigator would use chronometers as well as lunar distance methods to verify a vessel's longitude. The moon was reliable. Its mechanism would not break or run down (unlike a chronometer or a battery-powered GPS).

Maskelyne, an astronomer who had proved his method at sea, knew all that. He relied on that. He put generations of seamen in a position to capitalise on that by calculating lunar distance data and publishing it in the Nautical Almanac.

Sobel's book makes Maskelyne into a villain and I doubt that he was. His 'Mariner's Guide' is still a very good, clear read. His constancy, in publishing lunar distance data each year, from 1768 until his death, is remarkable. No computers in those days - no calculators, not even mechanical adding machines to help. Just pencils and lots and lots of paper. What a triumph! What an achievment! Almost the equal of Harrison's.

The Longitude Board messed about with Harrison in unforgivable ways, as Dava Sobel has recorded. He didn't get all the money he deserved for ages - in fact, it took a petition from the King and an Act of Parliament to achieve recognition for him and for his son, who took over his work.

But he eventually got more than £22,000 (several million in today's currency), from Parliament and the Longitude Board at the behest of the King himself.

Nevil Maskelyne became the Astronomer Royal but the Longitude Commissioners never awarded him a penny, despite the fact that his solution to the longitude question was viable and reliable and became the foundation stone of British naval power in the nineteenth century.

Harrison's chronometers (or the authorised copies of them which became the standard items carried on board British naval ships) were useless on very long voyages unless you could check them regularly with reference to lunar distance observations and calculations. This was long before Mr. Marconi had discovered how to broadcast time signals from Greenwich around the world. This was long before the ceremony of the 'noon gun' in Jersey, Hong Kong and Cape Town (and almost everywhere else where British ships called for trade, adventure and to protect British dominions and the Empire), a ceremony which allowed visiting ships to check and perhaps regulate their time pieces accurately before they moved on.

A chronometer, unless wound regularly and treated very, very carefully, will fail within a few days. A single chronometer, if you trust it wholeheartedly over a period of weeks and months, can develop an error and lead you seriously astray.

By the late nineteenth century, chronometers were cheap enough for a serious ocean going vessel to boast at least three. Claud Worth, a celebrated fore-runner of current cruising yachtsmen, relates in his book "Yacht Cruising" how a notice reading "have you wound the chronometers?" was placed on the breakfast table each morning on his yacht in the early twentieth century. Breakfast was not served unless the chronometers had been tended.

None of the clock-copies based on Harrison's chronometers would have survived the extended duration of Cook's voyages without being checked and rated by comparison with lunar distance observations, probably once or twice per month or towards the point of expected landfall.

Only by reference to lunar distance navigation and to Maskelyne's blue-print for it, was it possible to keep chronometers working effectively. And lunars (rather than chronometers) were the most crucial aid to navigation even when Richard Dana wrote, in the 1830s.

As Dana's ship approached Cape Horn, it was important to speak with another vessel, to learn where the ice was and to check longitude: "for we had no chronometer and had been drifting about so long that we had almost lost our reckoning; and opportunities for lunar observations are not frequent or sure in a place like Cape Horn."

Patrick O'Brian was, as everyone now knows, a fabulous chronicler of life at sea during the Napoleonic wars and he accurately tells of the exploits of British sailors when they tried to confront the elements, the enemy and the technologies of the time.

In his 'Blue at the Mizzen' (around page 148) two ships meet at sea and their Masters consult and quarrel about the longitude. One of them has lost the use of his chronometer. The phrase 'triangle of uncertainty' is used.

"There would be no problem," he says, "if I could only get a decent lunar."

But the skies have been cloudy. It was not the right time of the month.

(This incident is so very like one in Dana's 'Two Years before the Mast' that I wondered if O'Brian had cribbed it, as he copied and honourably re-invented many incidents from accounts in the Naval Gazette, of which he was a constant student.)

From Dana's book, again, around page 276:

"We had evidently made great progress and had good hope of being soon up with the Cape, if we were not there already. We could put but little confidence in our reckoning, as there had been no opportunities for an observation, and we had drifted too much to allow of our dead reckoning being anywhere near the mark. If it would clear off enough to give a chance for an observation, or if we could make land, we should know where we were; and upon these, and the chances of falling in with a sail from the eastward, we depended almost entirely."

What a world! What a way to live and sail, chancing everything on finding another vessel in the wastes of the Southern Ocean, risking a landfall on a barren, rocky coast, without any clear way of establishing - even within 100 miles - where you might be.

They were brave men, those sailors. No hot showers for them. No lavatories below the waterline. No breathable waterproof clothing or thermal underwear. Wickedly bad food, unyielding danger, the necessary disciplines of a ship at sea, the constant uncertainties about position, direction, landfall and survival.

Francis Chichester was a great and renowned airman before he became a renowned sailor and he taught and studied navigation for many years.

In his autobiography, The Lonely Sea And The Sky, he writes: (p. 297) "if one could rely on accurate information, navigation would be a simple science, whereas the art and great fascination of it lies in deducing correctly from uncertain clues."

In spite of Chichester's amazing knowledge of navigation, with the widest possible experience of teaching it, writing textbooks about it and using it as a flyer and as a seaman, in spite of his access or potential access to the most up-to-date Ocean Pilots, pilot charts and other reference sources, he is continually taken aback by ocean currents and eddies which upset his dead reckoning.

There are examples of his difficulties on pages 291 and 295 of his book and there are other, similar complaints elsewhere.

We are talking of 50 and more miles of error in a single day when dead reckoning has been carefully worked up by an acknowledged expert who spends up to two hours a day on his navigation, as he states on page 328 of the book.

This is very significant.

Chichester (p. 304) claims almost phenomenal expertise.

In particular, he says he can estimate the speed of his vessel to one quarter of a knot.

If Chichester could not get dead reckoning right all the time, then no one could or can.

Thank heaven for the Global Positioning System and its eventual successors. Long may they help to protect us from our own inefficiency on the oceans.

In May, 2,000, GPS SA (Selective Availability) was removed and GPS became suddenly much more accurate.

How kind of the American Government, which controls this system completely and unilaterally, to cease to degrade the signals and the system.

How very (apparently) warm-hearted!

from the Journal Of Navigation, Sept. 2001, p. 439

Selective Availability was removed because the "capacity to deny GPS signals on a regional basis was achieved at the beginning of 2000."

In other words, the Americans can switch GPS on or off, at any time, in any region of the world if they so choose.

Keep your sextants handy and practise dead reckoning whenever you can. I certainly intend to. You may need those skills one day.

*****

The author, braced for a noon sight

23/5 - Thursday

On Middle Watch. Six of us painfully and slowly furled the main course - in the dark, in the rain, in a fresh breeze (15-18 knots). Didn't turn a hair. No adrenalin rush at all - straight down from the yard, into my hammock - zonk! So much for physical danger as a stimulant. Motoring again - pitching sharply and unpleasantly. We will now definitely call at Cape Verde because we need more fuel.

24/5 - Friday

Still motoring grimly on! Teaching astro-navigation to George, Tony and Daniel . George's accuracy is excellent. He used to be a surveyor and is good at peering through small telescopes. The others are also better than I anticipated.

George trying a sextant for the very first time

25/5 - Saturday

Still motoring - course now 035 degrees (M).

Captain's Rounds.

Untired, (relatively) un-grumpy, un-fulfilled.

More astro tutorials with Daniel, Adam and Matt, who joined at Rio. Intercept errors equivalent to 2.5, 2 and 4 miles. Very satisfactory. George joined us. Between the five of us, we did 25 observations. George's best was just 25" off!

26/5 - Sunday

Layday - pleasantly cool last night - I slept on deck again. Another 'wine tasting' with Reg last night, a distraction from the routine and cheered us all up. Unfortunately, my palate for wine has gone completely - everything tastes like vinegar.

27/5 - Monday

0500 - taking over the stern watch

A grey dawn with the full moon still glaring down though wisps of grey cloud. Every day is different. Every dawn is individual. Close to us, the sea pants and pulses and throbs with its proper motions. At the horizon, as the light creeps past the clouds, it seems as still as stone.

28/5 - Tuesday

Up at 0400 yesterday, tired enough to sleep by 2200. Awake suddenly again at 0430 with the glorious illusion that we were sailing. Even the motion of the ship seemed to have changed and I could not hear the engines. I rushed to the hatchway in my boxers, climbed up, peered out and round. The growl of the engines assailed my ears. I was close to tears, as I am now, remembering the moment. We have been under power for more than five weeks.

28/5 - Tuesday (cont.)

1800 - approaching Cape Verde Islands - heroically twisted and jagged lava - formed rock formations down at the coast - a landscape as barren as the moon. Fort and fortifications on a little rock pinnacle to west of harbour entry. Portugese colonial relic? Could have dominated the whole anchorage with ease.

Later I was told that it had not, in fact, been a fort. I find that hard to believe.

Later still: a five-a-side football match under floodlights and some welcome hospitality afterwards.

At the football, everyone seemed to reinforce and re-present the characters that they present on board ship. Sarah (in goal) was stalwart, Ben (in attack) ran around incessantly and ineffectually but you had to admire him for his energy.

Alex and Tiff turned up so late they could not play (though they had talked up a storm beforehand). They were very effective in the bar.

Our opponents were, apparently, the Cape Verde championship team.

They certainly played like that. We didn't manage to score a single goal.

29/5 - Wednesday

Under engine heading for the Azores, which are 1,200 miles away. Glen used the word 'enjoy' in an announcement - he told us to 'sit back and enjoy the ride'.

Surely some mistake?

I am amused that my life on board now so much resembles my life on shore. Did I come all this way to be just the same? Here, I write verses quickly, read books greedily, keep notes obsessively, play the guitar sporadically, eat (always eagerly) and wash little but thoroughly. I might as well be on my canal boat in London.

But out here I do not drink alcohol and I work hard (physically) when there is hard physical work to be done.

I still have little sympathy for routine and no respect at all for authority however charming, young and disorganized the authority figure may be.

But it pleases me to be surrounded by younger people whom I admire, like and love.

I wish them so well.

The child and the man.

Martin's father was a statistician and academic. When Martin was young, he was made to add up and check some of his father's calculations.

"And then he would tell me how stupid I was if I got them wrong."

Martin is now 72 years old.

I could still hear the hurt in his voice.

30/5 - Thursday

Motoring again - will it ever stop? Getting off the ship to play football was a relief for everyone and I think we needed it.

"Everyone's gone flat," said Alf, the engineer.

Or perhaps he said "you've all gone flat."

Discovered an abandoned December copy of the New Scientist in the mess. Fell on it like a ravenous wolf - one article turned out to be about Rosalie David, who is still in Manchester working on Egyptian mummies - I wonder how Asru the Priestess of Amon is keeping?

Asru is an unwrapped mummy in the Manchester museum.

I made a film for the BBC called 'Everyday life in Ancient Egypt'. It was presented by Rosalie David. It was broadcast in 1983.

At one point we borrowed Asru from the Manchester museum and took her for an endoscopic examination at the local hospital.

Unfortunately, we forgot to take a sheet to cover her.

Wheeling her on a gurney through the corridors at the hospital, it was clear that her appearance - rather like a skeleton that had been fattened up a bit - was somewhat shocking to the visitors. She did look terribly naked.

I think she was about 2,500 years old at the time.

I couldn't help laughing, inside - it seemed very prudish to be offended by the nudity of such a very old lady.

The Brazilian biscuits are no more. A few crumbs at the bottom of a crumpled plastic bag testify to the illicit pleasure it gave me to have me own private and concealed source of refreshment and satisfaction.

I have been in Craig's company since February. I have never seen him angry or heard him criticise anyone or noticed that he is depressed or upset or ill. Is he a saint or something?

Now that it is really calm, the plumbing works. The heads are no longer awash with raw sewage, as they largely have been.

The engineers told me this plumbing was really designed and installed for a house and not for a boat - it didn't allow for all the rolling and pitching about. `

Starting yet another song; though it's the same tune I used at Rio there's probably going to be a different chorus:

> *So we turned the key and we got the engines running*
> *And we motored and we motored until all the fuel was done*
> *But we bought more fuel and the football it was stunning*
> *And we left the Verde Islands once the players' booze was gone*
>
> *Wey, hey, the wind and the rain*
> *We've forgotten how to sail Endeavour*
> *Hey, ho, this weather is a pain*
> *The engine's running better than ever*

31/5 - Friday

Rushing round interviewing everyone. I have it in mind to email some stories to local and national newspapers as we approach Whitby.

Interviews with Craig and Alex didn't reveal much - I think I know them both too well (and they know me.)

One of the more succesful interviews was with Vicky Paton who joined at Rio.

She was struck, she said, the minute she came on board by the fact that lifelong friendships had clearly been formed on the journey round Cape Horn.

That might have been daunting or off-putting but Vicky is good at getting on with people. I thought she really fitted in, even with the oldest of the old lags - Eddy and me.

Eddy's real name is Ingwar Guldner and he joined Endeavour at Hobart. He lives in Australia. He was a youthful looking 63 year old at that time, stocky and bearded, like someone from Scandinavia but still speaking with a noticeable German accent. A German film crew came on board to follow him around between Rio and Cape Verde.

Eddy emigrated to Australia when he was 19. He came alone to a brand new country. "I'm a loner," he says, without apology. "I like my own company."

He did not enjoy the lack of personal space and privacy on Endeavour.

"I would have liked to have some more of my own time (but) ... the cameraderie has been fantastic, absolutely fantastic ... I hardly knew anyone at first but how a mix of people from all ways of life, how they can get on cooped up in a boat like this that is only 33 metres, very close, so you can't get away from each other, no argument, no anger, 63 days together, just amazing. Terrific."

Eddy is an experienced sailor, with his own boat, a 43 foot sloop which he sailed for 15 years around Tasmania. He is also an adventurer, a risk-taker. Just before joining Endeavour, he was a convoy leader in Bosnia for the Red Cross.

"It was something new to do, something different, part of my own endeavour, to see the world," he says modestly.

"I was always interested in ships, any ships, especially tall ships, when I heard about this voyage, I said 'put my name down straight away' – Cape Horn was the Holy Grail for me. I'd read all about it for years, in books and I'm so happy I can still do this, at my age."

He didn't really feel the cold too much, he said, he had the right clothes and waterproofs. He shrugs off any discussion of the hardship and the physical endurance needed for the trip. Then he seems to contradict himself.

His fingers were bad, very bad – he says - he could never find a way to keep his fingers warm enough, especially when working aloft at night, furling the big, heavy wet main course in high winds with the ship rolling madly. He remembers one of those nights.

"Cold, wet and miserable, that was no fun – that was one of the low points - if someone had said to me, at that moment, do you want to go home, I'd have gone, at that moment."

Eddy noticed one of his watchmates who felt the cold even worse than him.

"If he could have cried, he would have cried," he said. "He had no circulation left in his hands."

Then, again, Eddy shrugs all memories of discomfort away.

Like most of us, he only remembers the excitement.

"Being under full sail, all the time, that was the big high for me. Days of it. And going round Cape Horn, that morning. Wonderful! You soon forget all the other stuff, all the bad stuff."

31/5 - Friday (cont.)

Flat calm, still motoring. At dusk, on stern watch, I had to sit down. While standing, I was strongly tempted to jump over the side just to break the monotony.
Claire the Penguin relieved me on stern watch.

"Beautiful seascape," I said.

To the west, the whole rim of the sky was ablaze with gold and red and full of puffy independent clouds, each with its purpose.

"I don't want to get there," she said guilelessly, as if from the heart.

Then she backtracked.

"I want to get to Whitby," she said, "Callan's going to be there, he's booked his ticket."

"I'm pleased for you," I said.

Callan is the boy friend. I know all about Callan.

I left it at that and went below for some sleep.

But I would have loved to have discussed that ambivalence - she wants to see Callan but she doesn't want to get there and get off - is that it?

I think I can identify with that.

*****

2/6 - Sunday

So I am spending my last few weeks on board looking round, looking at the people with whom I have spent the last months, transcribing the last of my notes, still trying to take stock, to work out what brought us all out here and who we really are.

My favourite people on board were Ruth and Martin Morant who had sailed more than 8,000 miles on Endeavour by that time.

Ruth was 68 years old, Martin celebrated his 72nd. birthday on that voyage. They have one daughter, Nicola, and, in 2002, they had just one grandchild, called Jack. They now have two.

Ruth is a very down to earth and unsentimental person but she carried pictures of her grandson with her on board the ship. She is always in charge of the couple's credit cards when they go ashore.

Ruth and Martin met racing Firefly dinghies at the University of London, where they were both students. She was the helm, he was the crewman. They were very successful, highly competitive until they moved to Durham in 1960, where Fireflies were not raced.

They gradually retired from racing but their interest in the sea and sailing grew even when they were off the water, concentrating on their careers and family affairs.

They eventually bought a cottage in Staithes, a village close to Whitby, and this led to an interest in the history of Captain Cook and the original Endeavour.

When the Endeavour replica came to Whitby in 1997, they visited it and heard about the possibility of taking passage. and Ruth led the way for both of them by sailing on Endeavour for four days between Hull and Plymouth in January 1998.

A much longer journey, between Hawaii and New Zealand, followed the same year and they have also crossed the Atlantic on another square rigged ship.

"It's a great adventure," says Martin, "to do this, to be part of it."

"I always wanted to know how square riggers sail," says Ruth briskly, as if it were the most normal thing in the world to spend almost a full year of her life finding this out by sailing most of the way round the world.

The current voyage on Endeavour is their longest passage yet and perhaps the most physically challenging.

They worried about that – about their health, about the cold, about the exertions necessary to survive on an old-fashioned wooden ship in the Southern Ocean.

Ruth and Martin do not undertake all of the work done by the voyage crew but Endeavour is not and never will be a comfortable or a cosy place to live. Life on board is fairly rugged even if you do not have to climb the masts and stand watch into the small hours of the mornings or undertake cleaning duties and maintenance for several hours each day.

Neither Ruth nor Martin is young or especially robust and Ruth is very small in stature. She is an unlikely figure on the quarter deck and she is completely dwarfed by the huge wheel, when she helms Endeavour. They inhabit the only double cabin in the stern of the ship, the officers' quarters. It is on a lower deck, below the waterline, and the sea water ran down the walls into their bedding in the Pacific and it was cold enough during the voyage for Ruth to get nasty chillblains.

When it was very rough, it was impossible to stay in their bunks and there was not enough space for both of them on the floor. Later on, crossing the Equator, when it was very hot, it was intolerable to stay in the cabin at all – they could have fried an egg on their mirror.

"Grim?" I suggested to Martin. "Weren't those conditions pretty grim?"

Martin is a very courteous man. Understatement is, for him, almost a way of life.

He thought the word 'grim' much too emphatic. "After all," he said, "the worst of it was only really for a very few days."

"You tell yourself that conditions aren't grim," said one of my watchmates later, "because you have to live in them."

Martin still climbs the masts regularly, though he doesn't have to, and he goes out on the yards and helps to furl and unfurl the big sails, the courses and topsails, when it is necessary.

Once Endeavour had her t'gallant masts aloft again, after she left the Pacific, he managed to get right to the top of the highest masts, as he did the last time he was on board Endeavour a few years ago.

Martin has grown his very first beard during the voyage — it is grey and bushy and patrician and he is not going to shave it off until his daughter has seen it and he has impressed his little grandson with his whiskers.

"Is it compulsory to have a beard on this ship?" asked a bright nine year old girl when the school parties visited the ship in New Zealand.

Certainly growing a beard is part of the Cape Horn experience for many. Perhaps the beard is part of the adventure for Martin, just as the hardship on board may be part of the attraction for some voyagers on Endeavour and the element of danger part of the fascination of sailing across a great ocean and round one of the most remote capes in the world in a replica of a vessel designed during the 1760s.

Ruth and Martin at Cape Horn

2/6 - Sunday (cont.)

Bright, sunny day - 20-25 knots on the nose and a fairly fierce chop with lots of water on deck and a pitching motion which is occasionally disconcerting. A layday, of course, like every Sunday, so everyone is relaxed and lazy, retreating into private space. Even Alex is strangely muted.

It is all very well for me to complain so much about motoring - how long would our passage have taken if we hadn't used the engines? Would we have been starving? Could we have carried enough fresh water to keep ourselves going if we hadn't been able to power up our generators and water-makers?

3/6 - Monday

Less than two weeks to go. Martin gave a talk about Whitby, our final destination, and Glen has made a map showing all the pubs and where we can get our photographs processed and buy kippers. I am thoroughly sick of all this. I want the journey to finish. The heads are flooded and stinking (again). The email doesn't work and I don't know what to write for which newspapers. I think the Channels have started - the old lags are certainly in a curious mood and I am ploughing through War and Peace with relish - that is always a distinct sign that I want to be elsewhere. It is the third time I have read it.

Yet I looked up at the rigging tonight (no square sails are set) - just the bare standing rigging and thought that, in less than three weeks, I will be off the ship and may never step on board her again and that thought was terrible to me. It breaks my heart.

6/6 - Thursday

Arrived Ponta Delgada 0830.

7/6 - Friday

On the quay at Ponta Delgada - last port before Whitby, last lot of newbies to come to terms with.

Emailed like mad yesterday - from one of the slowest email cafes in the world - it took me two hours to despatch just seven closely similar emails.

In one of them I referred (accidentally) to my feelings for people I have shared journeys with - "almost like love," I wrote.

Which brings to mind again Vicky's account of joining the ship where she says off-handedly "it was clear that lifelong friendships had been formed."

Martin touches on some of the same issues in his discussion of the psychology of sailing on the Endeavour web-site. So, after 5 months together, are we still all wondering why we came?

"I am proud to have been along," I wrote to my sons, "and grateful."

Grateful? A wholly unexpected adjective?
For the opportunity? For the companionship? For the health
and strength (and endurance) which has made it all possible?
Grateful? I wonder what on earth was in my head.
Perhaps it was the beauty.

THE RECKONING, STREAMING THE LOG

Everyone who has ever used a map or a chart probably knows about dead reckoning - but lots of people don't use maps any more and prefer SatNav or GPS. So a brief explanation of dead reckoning may be useful.

Dead reckoning is a simple calculation of speed and direction - you look at a map or chart, identify your starting point, then draw a line from your starting point in the direction you walked, sailed or motored. You establish your direction by using a compass.

How far along that line are you?

An easy calculation if you know your speed in miles per hour. Nowadays, there is no reason not to know your speed - whether walking, riding a bicycle or sailing, there are lots of ways to measure or to estimate your supposed speed and to estimate and guess how far you have travelled along that line of direction.

But in Captain Cook's day it was much more difficult, especially at sea. The only way of estimating speed was by streaming the log and this was a relatively skilled and relatively cumbersome operation.

The log (originally) was just that, a piece of wood which would float.

The principle is a simple one - if you drop the log overboard, it will stay in (roughly) the same place as the ship moves away from it. If you on board have retained a piece of string attached to the log, you can see how much string is pulled away from the ship in a given time and therefore calculate how fast you are going. Add a sandglass to measure the time taken to pull a given length of string off the boat and then you can use simple arithmetic to calculate your ship's speed through the water.

The string or light rope was calibrated by tying knots in it. Boat speed is still measured in knots rather than miles per hour.

The string was marked (every forty seven, forty eight or fifty feet - opinions differ) by a knot and you counted these knots to estimate the speed. I use the word 'estimate' and not the word 'measure' deliberately. Log lines of this type were not very accurate.

A retired naval officer who is a good friend asked me about the reason for 47 feet being used as the distance between knots (most text books say it should be fifty). I eventually worked it out and mailed him:

Hi, Ron,

Did some figuring with a calculator to confirm (to my own satisfaction) where the 47 foot divisions of the log line come from. I did the same while on board the Endeavour, but manually, on the back of an envelope, because we weren't supposed to be using our calculators, and that was a bit painful.

The nautical mile is 2026 yards, which is the circumference of the globe in land miles multiplied by 1760 to put it in yards, then divided by 360 degrees and 60 minutes.

As you know, 5 knots of boat speed = 5 nautical miles (10,130 yards which is 30,390 feet) in one hour.

Divide this down by 60 minutes and 60 seconds and by five and your result = 1.683333 feet per second; if you then multiply this fraction by 28", you should find that you need a measure of 47.273 feet for each knot.

You can also do the calculation for 30" but it is a slightly more difficult sum to do on paper and the result is likely to be a bit less accurate.

The 'log' on a modern vessel is much more sophisticated, the equivalent of a car's speedometer. It measures the boat's speed by a little propeller, which spins in the wake or is installed beneath the hull. The speed is displayed on a dial or computer screen. And, of course, GPS allows a vessel's speed <u>over the ground</u> to be checked, not just its speed through the water. GPS automatically allows for adverse currents or peculiar tidal streams.

N.A.M. Rodger confirms that there was no standard for log-lines in the middle of the eighteenth century, when Commodore Frankland petitioned the Admiralty to introduce one, claiming "dangerous variations in marking the log line ....." But nothing was done. No standard was established.

Everyone tied the knots in the log-line at different points, to compensate for differences in sand-glasses and for the nature of the vessels they sailed

I can imagine a Master, because it was the Master of a ship, not normally the Captain, who did the navigation, taking his favourite sandglass and, perhaps log-line from ship to ship, throughout his career, because consistency and reliability, would be more important (at that time) than real accuracy.

The charts were not accurate, so your measurements of distance travelled would also be approximate. But if your measurements/estimates were always consistent, that would be enormously advantageous.

During his first journey, Captain Cook, as recorded on p. 31, of the Penguin Edition of his Journals, had his log-line re-made off Patagonia, South America, after he had been at sea for several months, because the distances it measured did not conform to his estimates and his observations of latitude and his "account".

He complained about "a wrong division of the log line" which, he said, was "soon rectified." (The distance between each knot was two or more feet shorter than he required).

Eighteenth century sandglasses were sealed only with wax and could be adjusted, unlike the ones that were made for us on the BBC voyage. These were complete in glass and sealed and they seemed to vary hugely. We could not satisfactorily rate them and check them - the discrepancies were much larger than I would have expected.

Nicholas Blake is a considerable authority on these matters and the author, with Richard Lawrence, of 'The Illustrated Companion to Nelson's Navy'.

I consulted him about log lines before leaving to go on board Endeavour for the first time but his e-mail reply went astray and I only got it when I came back to London more than two months later.

Apparently, the log was streamed every hour on naval ships in unfamiliar waters (every two hours in known waters, near a known coastline). As Nick Blake says, Cook did not lack expert manpower. Every watchkeeper would probably have been capable of streaming the log and doing this every hour until close to land would not have been excessively demanding.

As Nick relates it, the officers of the watch would have been recording speed measured/estimated by the log, at least every hour.

We found streaming the log very demanding on the BBC voyage on Endeavour. We could only manage it once a day, almost for demonstration purposes. Only the navigators handled the log and there were only three of us and we were never normally on duty at the same time since we were attached to three different watches. This caused quite a few problems and one log was lost overboard as a result. That was when I started to try to work out exactly how far apart the knots should be, what the ideal timing should be and to wonder and to worry about the friction of the light rope which we were using. The weight of the line used and the friction as it ran off its big reel would clearly affect the accuracy of the results obtained by streaming the log. It did not matter on our brief BBC sponsored venture into the eighteenth century but it would have mattered enormously when Captain Cook was alive. But I am sure we could have allowed for it if we had to and if we had more time. We could have calculated how much friction mattered. I think those eighteenth century seamen were very pragmatic about what they did - it was not about theories or rules or calculations, it was about what seemed to work.

We also had trouble swinging the lead. We only had a relatively light weight (12 lbs., about 5.5 kg) and this lead tended to drag behind the vessel instead of finding bottom. This happened however expertly and vigorously Andy Law or one of the stronger young men on board sent it flying forward as you should when swinging the lead.

Cook, I believe, used huge heavy weights to establish his depth. Teams of twelve or more men (a whole watch) would have been organized to accomplish the operation. His lead probably weighed 50 or more pounds (20 kg or more.)

As Cook was entering the Channel, after his mammoth first voyage, in July 1771, he sounded in 60 fathoms (360 feet, more than 100 metres) and - just by the look of the seabed sample that the lead brought up - established that he was nearly home.

He didn't do that with a 12 lb. weight.

*****

COMING HOME

I didn't continue to keep a diary for the last 13 days of the trip.

Everything seemed to have been said.

Everything seemed to have ended.

Yet another set of 'newbies' came on board, including the very charming young Catherine Wood who trailed a film crew behind her like a royal entourage.

They filmed an interview with her in her hammock when I was half-asleep and I was tempted to rise up from mine and protest about the noise they were making.

Then I thought how I would look on camera, protesting from the shadows in the background of their shot, a half naked and still overweight old gentleman wearing boxer shorts and a sun-tan and a Commando hair cut, in a lousy temper, protesting about what they were doing ....

I put my pillow over my head and laughed at myself and tried to go to sleep - but I could still hear them messing about for what seemed like ages.

We called in at Alderney (a dull little island, where I had been many times before) and most of us got very drunk. The First Officer had told us not to drink at all because we were supposed to leave that same afternoon and we might have to climb the masts but we could see the Captain carousing in one of the pubs and we all went slightly mad.

We had earned it, I think.

Then the Captain declared a flat tyre and a lay over for the night and we went even madder.

To be in port in Alderney, introducing the young Australians to the sulky British way of life and food and weather was all that mattered. It was a very grey day but I went on the beach and wandered and pondered and took photographs of Ruth and Martin.

We were still motoring. We had been motoring most of the way north in the Atlantic. As we ploughed up the Channel past places I knew, places where I had learned to sail, it was terrifying and tempting to think of the journey coming to an end. But I had had enough. I think we all had.

Exhaustion and the infinite tension and monotony of a long, long journey - I wanted an end to come.

I occupied myself with writing, interviewing, considering and recording the nature of the people with whom I had shared my life with for almost six months - Sarah, Andy, Craig, Alex, Kate, Ruth and Martin and so many others. I was still interested in the people, still positive about them, however pissed off I felt about the situation.

As we came closer and closer to Whitby, there were helicopters and light aeroplanes filming us, there were boats full of tourists and cameramen coming out to us.

It was an extraordinary atmosphere, humbling and emotional and a great tribute to the ship and to the people who sail her.

I am very proud to have been part of that. A small part. An insignificant part. They could definitely have done it without me.

But I was there.

I always wanted, from many years ago, to sail round Cape Horn. I always thought that I would have to do it single handed, to sell up in the U.K., take the money I could raise to New Zealand, buy a tough little boat there and fit it out and then sail it single handed to the east until I had reached the Atlantic again.

I don't have to do that now and I am glad. Single handers babble. (I would make an alarmingly good single hander. I babble quite a lot.) They talk and cannot listen. I no longer want to sail single-handed, though the challenge might still seduce me, in the end.

The friends I have made while sailing have been by far the most important elements of the experience - old friends, young friends, eccentric friends, beautiful friends, it is the people that count.

Never more so than when we arrived at Whitby surrounded by a flotilla, firing off our cannon as often as we could, slipping through the piers that flank the narrow entrance to the harbour, with kayaks paddling dangerously close alongside us and about 100,000 people on the cliffs cheering and shouting and welcoming us home.

We had sailed half way across the globe and we had made it on time. On the due date, 21st. June 2002.

Only a few of the voyage crew had come the whole way - Alex, Craig, Clare, Claire, Graham, Graeme, Kevin, Jon, me - who else? Who have I forgotten? Pete the Fish (though technically he joined at Hobart) - oh stupid me, Nigel Longster. Ruth and Martin. There are still more names to include Tiffany and GI Jane - though they didn't come quite the whole way. I cannot think of that day and those people without crying, which is exactly as it should be. I am crying as I write this.

And then my children.

I was in the waist of the ship, starboard side, helping to heave a huge fender over the side of the ship with four or five other people.

I was wondering how many of my children could have got to Whitby, who would meet me, I was just thinking of them. And we lifted the fender and rolled it over the gunwale and I looked up at the shore and there he was, pointing at me, grinning at me - the biggest grin you ever saw - my second son, Matthew.

He seemed almost close enough for me to touch him. Beside him, for God's sake I could see them, I could recognize them - my other three sons. All of them. It was a wonderful, wonderful moment. I had to get on with the work and make fast the fender and get the jackstaff up the bowsprit. I couldn't cry then at the beauty of that moment, the excitement of it - the sheer joy.

But it was wonderful!

I have made up for it this evening, just while writing this account. A lot of tears have been shed this evening.

Later, we moored up and I stepped ashore. Dan and Amanda were there as well, the young couple with whom I had sailed the Indian Ocean. I couldn't believe it. All my favourite people! Only my daughter, a music student in Manchester, couldn't make it.

Joshua gave me a huge hug. Barnaby hugged me and very discreetly slipped me a hip flask full of Irish whiskey. Later on, I showed them round the ship. It was a great pleasure to take a swig from the hip flask in the Great Cabin where I had so often had to polish the furniture. I think I probably also took a swig in the lavatories, which I had cleaned a few hundred times.

The first phone call for me, on Ben's mobile phone, was from Ann Hay, my former wife, his mother. She has a lovely voice. She had re-married by then and is, I think, quite happy with the different directions in which our lives have gone.

But she still has a beautiful voice. I once wrote that she was 'beautiful from the inside', as Amanda is also.

I was very pleased indeed to get that phone call.

The day after I got back, we all went out for lunch at an attractive hotel and restaurant outside Whitby, up on the moors. I can remember very little about it. I was exhausted and so full of memories I had no room for more.

I suppose I ate. I suppose I drank. I have no idea.

All I remember is the beauty of the peacock strutting the lawn and the heady joy of being with friends and family again.

"Incorrigibly plural" wrote Louis MacNeice about the world. "Incorrigibly plural." And he wrote a very famous poem about snow outside his window and rich red roses inside and a warm, warm fire.

The contrast between my life on board Endeavour and the genteel ordered beauty of that restaurant's gardens was unbelievable.

The contrast between the savage beauty of the Southern Ocean waves, the cold tranquillity of the stars at night, the billowing sails in sunshine and the English roses in the borders was overwhelming.

The tension between the endless routine watches on board, the grinding labour, the wonderful innocent companionship of the young people and the thought of returning to bourgeois values, chats with the bank manager, unlimited leisure, my ordinary urban life made me reel with dizziness and confusion.

It takes months to recover from a journey of this sort. Perhaps I never have.

I returned humbler, thinner, more aware of my own shortcomings, heartened by new friendships, inspired by love and a sense of achievment which gave me great hope.

Did it change me? Was it a life changing experience?

It was certainly life-enhancing. It made more of me. I am more me because of it.

To grow into yourself, with all your flaws and weaknesses and peculiarities, is all that a human being can ever hope to achieve.

To become the person you are to the utmost degree.

"Das ist ein Mensch" is a German-Jewish saying - a great compliment.

"That is a real human being."

I hope I am a real human being, more so because of Endeavour, but that is for others to judge.

Whenever I run away to sea or lose myself in hard work, alcohol or exertion I never forget another saying, attributed to St. Augustine.

"Whither shall I flee, that I shall flee myself?"

We all must bear an identical burden, face up to an identical responsibility.

To be ourselves.

The room was suddenly rich and the great bay-window was

Spawning snow and pink roses against it

Soundlessly collateral and incompatible:

World is suddener than we fancy it.

World is crazier and more of it than we think,

Incorrigibly plural. I peel and portion

A tangerine and spit the pips and feel

The drunkenness of things being various.

"Snow"- by Louis Macneice - an extract

THE LAST WORD

(The text of a lecture at the conference to celebrate the 25th. anniversary of the Raising of the Mary Rose, October 2007)

I took part in the BBC tv series about Endeavour as one of the team of navigators, working and living under something close to eighteenth century conditions, and I then signed on as an ordinary crew member. I helped to sail Endeavour from Fremantle, in Western Australia, to Whitby, in Yorkshire, around Cape Horn. I spent 166 days at sea on Endeavour in twelve months, pondering almost every day on the extraordinary skills of the old navigators and the extraordinary difficulty of what they did.

It is supposed to be easy, nowadays, to know both where you are at sea and what you are most likely to bump in to. But, as the fate of H.M.S. Nottingham shows - she was a British destroyer that whacked Wolf Rock, near Australia, in 2002 - the sea is still a very dangerous place.

In the eighteenth century, especially in the early years of that century, you never knew exactly where you were and you had very little chance of working out what you would bump in to from the primitive charts and navigational handbooks that were available.

Explorers before Cook sailed round the world relied on the three Ls - 'lead, lookout and latitude' to keep their ships safe.

"Lead' - you swing the lead, dropping a lump of lead on a piece of string over the side of the ship, to find the depth. If the water is getting shallow very quickly, you try to go somewhere else immediately (if the wind happens to be in the right direction). But if you are approaching Boston (see Dana's great book, 'Two Years before the Mast',) you can navigate yourself into port in a fog by the samples of the sea-bottom that the tallow in a recess of the lead weight picks up and brings to the surface.

'Lookout' - while you are out at sea, you are safe (except from the elements) - it is the proximity of land which is frightening and brings you into the most extreme danger - so (if you are an old-time navigator) you post good lookouts all the time - especially when the water starts to get shallow. The lookouts can spot the tell-tale patch of cloud on the horizon that indicates a Pacific island, they can (if you are lucky) tell you when the colour of the water changes, which shows that you are getting closer to land; also, they can observe the type of birds that are seen, note the re-appearance of flies on board, maybe they notice a flying cockroach or catch a glimpse of a butterfly - there are lots of indicators that land is near that a good lookout can detect.

'Latitude' - from Phoenician times and certainly from medieval times, people knew that the Pole Star ('our star' as it is described in Dante's Inferno, written in 1320) was a good means of navigation.

It tells you where north is, in approximate terms, but also, if you measure or estimate its angle, it tells you how far up or down the globe you are, that is to say it establishes your latitude. People have relied on it as a basic indicator of geographical position for a very very long time. The sun at noon fulfils the same function, if you know how to use it, what allowances to make, which season (and which hemisphere) you are in.

Measuring angles is important for old-style navigation. It is the angle of the sun or of a star, in relation to the horizon or in relation to another heavenly body, which enables you to hypothesize where you might be, to make a well-informed guess about your vessel's whereabouts.

Whenever I get my sextant out on land, probably to check it, someone will always come up and make the jocular comment: "Where are we then? Know where we are?"

I try to be polite, but it always enrages me.

Sextants never tell you where you are. They are not like GPS at all - I love my sextant dearly but it is essentially a jumped up protractor just like the plastic gadgets children use at school but fabricated very accurately in metal and fitted with optics and micrometers and heavy filters to allow you to look directly at the sun - Sextants Measure Angles. That is all that they do.

What you do with the angles (afterwards) is up to you. You can use nineteenth century techniques (Sumner's position line/Marq St. Hilaire) which ought to allow you to calculate your position to within 2-5 miles from your true position or you can use the eighteenth century lunar distance methods that Captain Cook knew and Nevil Maskelyne (demonised as Harrison the Chronometer's worst enemy in Dava Sobel's book, 'Longitude') pioneered. This will give you your longitude "within a degree or a little more" as Maskelyne ventured in his introduction to "The British Mariner's Guide' published in 1763.

It will also take you hours and hours of patient calculation.

A degree of longitude is 60 miles at the equator. Maskelyne's method could produce a 'circle of uncertainty' around 75 miles wide, a vast improvement on the status before Maskelyne got to work, when the 'circle of uncertainty' could be hundreds of miles in diameter.

On the BBC voyage, my colleagues and I seem to have done rather better than Maskelyne predicted. Comparing the GPS positions of the ship with our estimates of its position after the journey showed that we were generally accurate to rather less than a degree. However, we had clear skies and very calm conditions.

On my second voyage on Endeavour, on the way across the Pacific, from Bluff, in New Zealand, to Cape Horn, Endeavour didn't see the sun or any star at all for 18 of the 39 days before we reached Cape Horn. We were also driven north (hove to) for a day and a half by a big storm. If I had been navigating by sextant and dead reckoning alone, I would have been a very worried man because it was impossible to tell, within a hundred or more miles, even what latitude we were on.

What have I learned? I have spent almost 12 months studying and working with eighteenth century ships and eighteenth century navigational techniques. What have I proved or learned or established?

James Cook deserves his fame and his glory. His journeys are like the sculptures of Michelangelo - inimitable, unique, masterly, beautiful. When his men died from malaria, on the first voyage, he wrote about each of them as a friend; when his ship was in danger on the Barrier Reef, he records it in his journal with huge sang-froid and a professionalism which freezes my blood. He brought his ships and people home - not just on the first journey but then again on the second. His untimely death, on the third journey, was a sad and unnecessary tragedy - he was trying to prevent an escalation of a violent clash between the natives of Hawaii and his heavily armed supporters. But his men and his ships got home, even without him.

When Cook was 25 years old, his employer in Whitby (a Mr. Walker) expected him to become the skipper of one of the Walker colliers trading from Whitby to Newcastle and then to London. It was, I think, a good professional opportunity. Cook would have been secure and prosperous for life and he had started as a farm labourer's son with an apparent future just as a labourer or a shop-keeper.

Cook chose instead to join the British Navy as an able seaman. He wanted to learn more about the world and he did. He taught himself surveying, navigation, seamanship, man-management. He saw himself as more than just a collier's skipper, more than just an ordinary person.

He felt he had an important future in the wider world and he turned out to be right.

He was a great, great man and having, hesitantly and nervously, followed in some of his footsteps, I am more impressed than ever by his expertise, his energy and his capacity to endure.

The ship (the Endeavour replica) represents some of that and communicates some of it to you when you go on board.

Have a look at her, if you ever can - it is a wonderful experience. People like me, who have sailed on board, fall in love with Endeavour entirely and return repeatedly to find out more about her and about Captain James Cook.

It could be your turn next, to climb a mast or two, in gusty winds.

You won't ever forget the experience, if you do.

Captain Cook's return home is worth recalling in detail, in his own words.

> Wednesday, 10th (July, 1771). Pleasant breezes and Clear weather. At 6 o'Clock in the Morning sounded, and Struck ground in 60 fathoms Shells and Stones, by which I judged we were the length of Scilly Isles. At Noon we saw land from the Mast Head, bearing north, which we judged to be about the Land's End. Soundings 54 fathoms, Coarse, Grey Sand. Wind westerly; course north 44 degrees east; distance 97 miles; latitude 49 degrees 29 minutes north, longitude 6 degrees 18 minutes west.

Twenty four hours later, they encountered "a fresh Gale, with which we run briskly up Channel."

Briskly indeed - I estimated his speed by his account of the landmarks on shore and it seems that Captain James Cook and his crew, the veterans of one of the great voyages, who should have been exhausted, debilitated, ravaged with scurvy, whose ship should have been on its last legs and riddled with worm, covered the last 175 nautical miles in a magnificent 21. 5 hours - a speed of more than 8 knots. They probably had a big tide with them for more than half the time but it must still have been great sailing. Both foremast and main courses? The foremast topsail? Which of the spritsails? He doesn't say. Two strong men on the wheel - the ship flying home as if she wanted to, the deck bucking underfoot, everyone inwardly terrified and tearful and trembling with anticipation at the thought of stepping again, alive, having survived that epic adventure onto the soil of their homeland.

I think I now know how they felt.

THE END

ACKNOWLEDGEMENTS

Friends who read the book in manuscript or helped in other ways are, in alphabetical order:

David Aukin, Nick Blake, Gareth Edwards, Mark Eisenthal, Leonie Flood, David Floyd, Katya Gerasimova-Bosky, Barnaby Gilbert, Judy Head, David McGovern, Ruth and Martin Morant, Will Nelson, Jon Preston, Dan and Amanda Schnurr.

My warmest thanks to all of them.

In the section which follows this page:

Details of Endeavour's sail plan were derived from the Australian National Maritime Museum web-site.

The plan showing all the lines on board comes from an Endeavour Foundation introductory pamphlet.

Details of Endeavour's crew are reproduced from research originated by the University of Adelaide.

Grateful acknowledgements to the National Maritime Museum for permission to reproduce the engraving of James Cook on page 14.

The extract from Louis MacNeice's poem, "Snow" is reproduced by kind permission of David Higham Associates; the poem is published in full by Faber & Faber in MacNeice's Collected Poems.

All but two photographs in this book were scanned from the original negatives created by the author They are copyright and must not be reproduced without written permission. Cameras used on board Endeavour - Minox GT and Nikon F60. Photographic film - Kodak Gold 200. Processing by Boots (C41), scanned to digital with the Nikon Coolpix Scanner. Photoshop CS3 to finish.

GLOSSARY

Bark - the words 'schooner' and 'ketch' signify precisely how many masts and what type of masts a yacht or ship carries. But the words 'bark', 'barque' and 'barquentine' had several different and confusing meanings between the eighteenth and nineteenth centurries.

Endeavour, an adapted collier, is sometimes described as a 'Whitby cat;' or as a cat-headed bark, but she was called 'The Bark Endeavour' in Admiralty documents primarily because of Captain Cook's rank (Lieutenant) when he started his first famous journey. If he had been more senior, she might have been classified as a sloop; according to details on the Australian National Maritime Museum web-site, a bark called Resolution was designated as a 'sloop' on his second and third voyages. by which time he was ranked as a Commander.

Endeavour has three masts (as barks normally did) and the hull shape of a bark (flat bow, square stern) but she carries a square rigged topsail on her mizzen mast - a bark, at least as defined later on, in the nineteenth century, carried only fore and aft sails on the mizzen mast.

Cleats - the big wooden double hooks on which lines are secured.

Fore mast, fore course - the fore-mast is at the front of the ship. The fore course is the biggest and lowest sail on that mast.

Haversines - The 'horrible haversines' (mentioned in passing) are a means of resolving spherical trigonometry problems associated with navigational techniques without using a computer or calculator.

Hove to - The ship's sails and the rudder are made to contradict each other so that the ship points into the wind and drifts backwards.

Idlers - member of the crew who do not stand watches every day and every night because they are specialist carpenters, riggers or cooks.

Main mast, main course - the mast in the middle of the ship. The biggest and lowest sail on that mast.

Mizzen mast, mizzen course (aka driver or spanker) - the mast at the stern of the ship. The lowest of the sails on that mast.

Navigation techniques - including lunar distance, the Marq St. Hilaire method, the Sumner position line etc. Eighteenth and nineteenth century methods of using the measured angles of the sun or stars to calculate the approximate longitude of a ship at sea.

Preventers - when sailing, some sails need to be tied back to stop them causing trouble if the wind gets behind them. The lines used for this are called 'preventers'. When wearing or tacking the ship, the preventers need to be cast off and it can be inconvenient or even dangerous if this does not happen on cue.

Staysails - this book is too short to include much detail about sails and rigging. Briefly, the main sails on a square rigger are the big square sails hung from 'yards' (big bits of timber) on each of the masts. The staysails are the fore and after sails between the masts.

Supernumeraries - passengers on Endeavour who may also join a watch and help with the running of the ship.

T'gallants - top gallants, the very highest masts and sails; they can be taken down when the ship prepares to venture into really fierce conditions in, for example, the Southern Ocean.

Voyage crew - volunteers who pay for their berths and undertake all the hard physical labour on board the Endeavour replica.

Wearing ship - turning the ship away from the wind and steering it in a circle to bring the wind onto the other side of the vessel. It achieves the same result as tacking but you are turning the stern of the ship through the wind instead of the bow and it is much kinder on the rigging of a square rigger, which is designed primarily to withstand forces from the stern. It takes a lot longer than tacking a modern yacht and involves most of the crew and a large number of laborious sail adjustments. You also need a lot of sea room.

*****

THE SAIL PLAN OF ENDEAVOUR The sail area is approximately 10,000 sq feet (930 m2)

On bowsprit
* 1. Spritsail topsail 467 sq ft (43.38 m2)
* 2. Spritsail 435 sq ft (40.41 m2)
* 3. Jib 468 sq ft (43.39 m2)
* 4. Fore top stay sail 384 sq ft (35.67 m2)

Foremast
* 5. Fore course 840 sq ft (78.04 m2)
* 6. Fore topsail 989 sq ft (91.87 m2)
* 7. Fore t'gallant 467 sq ft (43.38 m2)

Between Fore & Main
* 8. Main topmast staysail 630 sq ft (58.53 m2)
* 9. Main t'gallant staysail 450 sq ft (41.8 m2)
* 10. Main staysail 431 sq ft (40.04 m2) - THE WORST SAIL IN THE WORLD TO FURL!

Mainmast
* 11. Main course 1197 sq ft (110.74 m2)
* 12. Main topsail 404 sq ft (37.53 m2)
* 13. Main t'gallant 519 sq ft (48.22 m2)

Between Main & Mizzen
* 14. Mizzen staysail 85 sq ft (7.9 m2)
* 15. Mizzen topmast staysail 155 sq ft (14.4 m2)

Mizzenmast
* 16. Mizzen course (driver) 308 sq ft (28.6 m2)
* 17. Mizzen topsail 643 sq ft (59.73 m2)

THE SAILS AND LINES ON ENDEAVOUR

The sail plan and the location of the lines on Endeavour would have conformed to the standard patterns on other Royal Navy ships of the time. There was nothing strange or surprising about the Endeavour's rig to Captain Cook's original crew. To us, of course, it is a mystery.

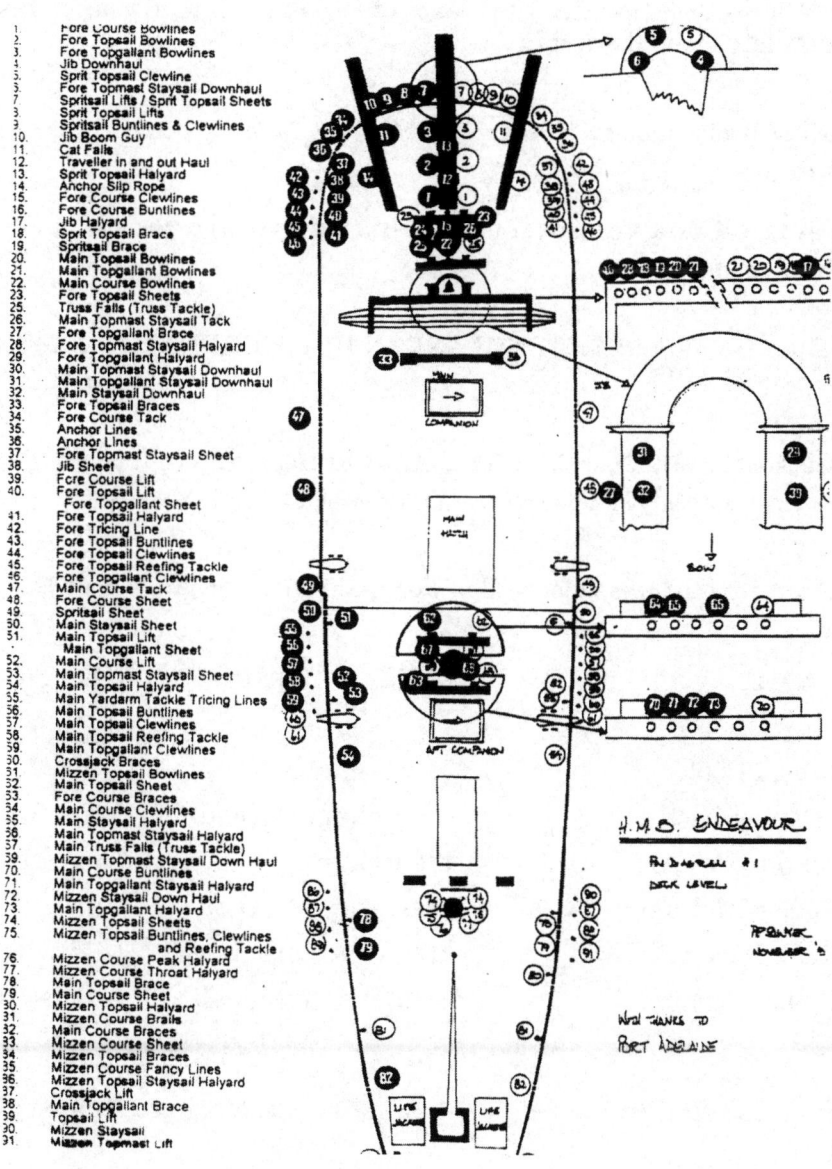

1. Fore Course Bowlines
2. Fore Topsail Bowlines
3. Fore Topgallant Bowlines
4. Jib Downhaul
5. Sprit Topsail Clewline
6. Fore Topmast Staysail Downhaul
7. Spritsail Lifts / Sprit Topsail Sheets
8. Sprit Topsail Lifts
9. Spritsail Buntlines & Clewlines
10. Jib Boom Guy
11. Cat Falls
12. Traveller in and out Haul
13. Sprit Topsail Halyard
14. Anchor Slip Rope
15. Fore Course Clewlines
16. Fore Course Buntlines
17. Jib Halyard
18. Sprit Topsail Brace
19. Spritsail Brace
20. Main Course Bowlines
21. Main Topgallant Bowlines
22. Main Course Bowlines
23. Fore Topsail Sheets
25. Truss Falls (Truss Tackle)
26. Main Topmast Staysail Tack
27. Fore Topgallant Brace
28. Fore Topmast Staysail Halyard
29. Fore Topgallant Halyard
30. Main Topmast Staysail Downhaul
31. Main Topgallant Staysail Downhaul
32. Main Staysail Downhaul
33. Fore Topsail Braces
34. Fore Course Tack
35. Anchor Lines
36. Anchor Lines
37. Fore Topmast Staysail Sheet
38. Jib Sheet
39. Fore Course Lift
40. Fore Topsail Lift
    Fore Topgallant Sheet
41. Fore Topsail Halyard
42. Fore Tricing Line
43. Fore Topsail Buntlines
44. Fore Topsail Clewlines
45. Fore Topsail Reefing Tackle
46. Fore Topgallant Clewlines
47. Main Course Tack
48. Fore Course Sheet
49. Spritsail Sheet
50. Main Staysail Sheet
51. Main Topsail Lift
    Main Topgallant Sheet
52. Main Course Lift
53. Main Topmast Staysail Sheet
54. Main Topsail Halyard
55. Main Yardarm Tackle Tricing Lines
56. Main Topsail Buntlines
57. Main Topsail Clewlines
58. Main Topsail Reefing Tackle
59. Main Topgallant Clewlines
60. Crossjack Braces
61. Mizzen Topsail Bowlines
62. Main Topsail Sheet
63. Fore Course Braces
64. Main Course Clewlines
65. Main Staysail Halyard
66. Main Topmast Staysail Halyard
67. Main Truss Falls (Truss Tackle)
69. Mizzen Topmast Staysail Down Haul
70. Main Course Buntlines
71. Main Topgallant Staysail Halyard
72. Mizzen Staysail Down Haul
73. Main Topgallant Halyard
74. Mizzen Topsail Sheets
75. Mizzen Topsail Buntlines, Clewlines and Reefing Tackle
76. Mizzen Course Peak Halyard
77. Mizzen Course Throat Halyard
78. Main Topsail Brace
79. Main Course Sheet
80. Mizzen Topsail Halyard
81. Mizzen Course Brails
82. Main Course Braces
83. Mizzen Course Sheet
84. Mizzen Topsail Braces
85. Mizzen Course Fancy Lines
86. Mizzen Topsail Staysail Halyard
87. Crossjack Lift
88. Main Topgallant Brace
89. Topsail Lift
90. Mizzen Staysail
91. Mizzen Topmast Lift

229

CAPTAIN COOK'S CREW

It was oddly difficult to establish exactly how many people sailed with Captain Cook on his first voyage and how many survived the experience.

To my delight, I eventually found that the University of Adelaide had made the text of Cook's journals and his complete crew list available:

http://ebooks.adelaide.edu.au/c/cook/james/c77j/crew.html

Captain Cook's Journal during his first voyage round the world

PERSONS WHO LEFT ENGLAND IN H.M.S. ENDEAVOUR, 26TH AUGUST, 1768.

Rendered into HTML on Mon Jun 23 17:37:10 2003, by Steve Thomas for The University of Adelaide Library Electronic Texts Collection.

Those not otherwise disposed of were paid off on 1st August, 1771.

NAME	RANK	DISPOSAL & DATE
James Cook	Lieutenant in Command.	
Zachary Hicks	Lieutenant	Died 25 May, 1771.
John Gore	Lieutenant.	
Robert Molineux	Master	Died 15 April, 1771.
Rich. Pickersgill	Master's Mate, Master, 16 April, 1771.	
Chas. Clerke	Master's Mate, A.B., 20 August, 1768, Master's Mate, 17 April, 1771, Lieutenant, 26 May, 1771.	
Francis Wilkinson	A.B., Master's Mate, 20 August, 1768.	

John Bootie	Midshipman Died 4 February, 1771.
Jonathan Monkhouse	Midshipman Died 6 February, 1771.
Patrick Saunders	Midshipman, A.B., 24 May, 1770
	Deserted 25 December, 1770.
Isaac Smith	A.B., Midshipman, May, 1770,
	Master's Mate, 27 May, 1771
William Harvey	Lieutenant's Servant, Midshipman,
	8 February, 1771.
Jos. Magra	A.B., Midshipman, 27 May, 1771.
Isaac Manley	Master's Servant, Midshipman,
	5 February, 1771.
William B. Monkhouse	Surgeon Died 5 November, 1770.
William Perry	Surgeon's Mate, Surgeon,
	6 November, 1770.
Rich. Orton	Clerk.
Stephen Forwood	Gunner.
John Gathray	Boatswain Died 4 February, 1771.
John Satterly	Carpenter Died 12 February, 1771.
John Thompson	Cook Died 31 January, 1771.
Sam Evans	Quarter Master, Boatswain,
	6 February, 1771.
Alex. Weir	Quarter Master Drowned
	14 September, 1768.
Thos. Hardman	Boatswain's Mate, A.B., 26 March, 1769,
John Reading	Boatswain's Mate
	Died 29 August, 1769.
Benjamin Jordan	Carpenter's Mate
	Died 31 January, 1771.
John Ravenhill	Sailmaker Died 27 January, 1771.
George Nowell	A.B., Carpenter, 14 February, 1771.
Isaac Parker	Boatswain's Mate, 26 November, 1769.

Robt. Anderson	A.B., Quarter Master, 16 September, 1768.
James Gray	A.B., Quarter Master, 6 February, 1771.
Robert Taylor	Armourer Died 1 August, 1771.
Rich. Hutchins	A.B., Boatswain's Mate, 1 September, 1769.
Joseph Childs	A.B., Cook, 1 February, 1771.
Peter Flowers	A.B. Drowned 2 December, 1768.
Timothy Rearden	A.B. Died 24 December, 1770.
John Rainsay	A.B.
William Dawson	A.B.
Francis Haite	A.B. Died 1 February, 1771.
Sam Jones.	A.B.
James Nicholson	A.B. Died 31 January, 1771.
Forby Sutherland	A.B. Died 30 April, 1770.
Thomas Simmonds	A.B.
Rich. Hughes	A.B. Carpenter's Mate, 14 February, 1771.
Sam Moody	A.B. Died 31 January, 1771.
Isaac Johnson	A.B.
Robt. Stainsby	A.B.
William Collett	A.B.
Archibald Wolfe	A.B. Died 31 January, 1771.
Matthew Cox	A.B.
Chas. Williams	A.B.
Alex. Simpson	A.B.. Died 21 February, 1771.
Thos. Knight	A .B.
Hy. Stevens	A.B.
Thos. Jones (2)	A.B.
Antony Ponto	A.B.

Jeh. Dozey	A.B. Died 7 April, 1771.
Jas. Tunley	A.B.
Mich. Littleboy	A.B.
John Goodjohn	A.B.
John Woodworth	A.B. Died 24 December, 1770.
William Peckover	A.B.
Robt. Littleboy	A.B.
Henry Jeffs	A.B. Died 27 February, 1771.
William Howson	Captain's Servant Died 30 June, 1771.
Nathl. Morey	Lieutenant's Servant.
Thos. Jones	Surgeon's Servant Discharged 5 November, 1770.
Ed. Terrell	Carpenter's Servant, A.B. Died 1 September, 1769.
Thos. Jordan	Boatswain's Servant.
Thos. Matthews	Cook's Servant.
Danl. Roberts	Gunner's Servant Died. 2 February, 1771.
John Thurmand	(Pressed at Madeira). A.B., Died 3 February, 1771.

MARINES

John Edgecombe	Sergeant R.M.
John Trusslove	Corporal Died 24 January, 1771.
Thos. Rossiter	Drummer.
William Judge	Private.
Hy. Paul	Private.
Danl. Preston	Private Died, 16 February, 1771.
William Wiltshire	Private.
William Greenslade	Private Drowned, 6 April, 1769.

Saml. Gibson	Corporal, Died 26 January, 1771.
Thos. Dunster	Private, Died 26 January, 1771.
Clement Webb	Private.
John Bowles	Private.

CIVILIANS AND STAFF

Joseph Banks, Esquire.	
Charles Solander	Naturalist.
Charles Green	Astronomer Died 29 January, 1771.
John Reynolds	Artist Died 18 December, 1770.
Sydney Parkinson	Artist Died 26 January, 1771.
Alexander Buchan	Artist Died 17 April, 1769.
Herman Sporing	Died 24 January, 1771.
James Roberts	Servant.
Peter Briscoe	Servant.
Thomas Richmond	Negro Servant, Frozen to death 16 January, 1769.
George Dorlton	Negro Servant, Frozen to death 16 January, 1769.

TOTAL LOSS

1768   Drowned 2.

1769   Drowned 1.

1769   Frozen 2.

1769   Died 2.

1770   Died 5.

1771   Died 26.

Total   38.